EXCLUSIVE SIGNED EDITION

Love
Pippa x

PIPPA O'CONNOR ORMOND

October 2019

PENGUIN

IRELAND

THE
PIPPA GUIDE

To Jenny, my friend & mentor.
I'll always be inspired by you.
Thank you for everything.
1977–2019 x

THE
PIPPA GUIDE

Live Your Best Life

PIPPA O'CONNOR ORMOND

PENGUIN

IRELAND

PENGUIN IRELAND

UK | USA | Canada | Ireland | Australia
India | New Zealand | South Africa

Penguin Ireland is part of the Penguin Random House
group of companies whose addresses can be found at
global.penguinrandomhouse.com.

Penguin
Random House
UK

First published 2019
001

Copyright © Pippa O'Connor Ormond, 2019

The moral right of the copyright holders has been asserted

Design by Hart Studio

Cover photo by Laoise Moggan

Photography by Pippa O'Connor Ormond: pp. 29, 45, 54, 93, 204, 106,
134, 148, 196, 202, 208, 213, 214, 220, 225, 226, 237, 240, 243, 249,
263, 266, 269.

Lili Forberg: pp. 57, 67, 69, 70, 71, 72, 74, 76, 77, 79, 80, 83, 85, 86, 90,
94, 99, 100, 102, 103, 112, 113, 115, 120, 124, 127, 128, 130, 133, 155,
157, 160, 165, 166, 173, 177.

Laoise Moggan: pp. 6, 7, 8, 15, 16, 18, 20, 23, 25, 31, 34, 41, 59, 138,
139, 140, 141, 142, 143, 145, 196, 250, 272.

Brian McEvoy: p. 34.

Barry McCall: p. 143.

Kieran Harnett: p. 266.

Colour reproduction by Born Group

Printed and bound by Firmengruppe APPL, aprinta druck, Wemding,
Germany

A CIP catalogue record for this book is available from the British Library

ISBN: 978-1-844-88473-5

CONTENTS

Hello,

Isn't life funny these days? We all see so much of everyone's life on social media, it's easy to think you know everything about them. If you follow me on Instagram or have been to one of our Fashion Factories you probably do know a lot – I mean, a lot of you know that I mixed up PayPal accounts last February so that Brian ended up buying his own Valentine's Day present (embarrassing yes, but way too funny not to share)!

So, when we were talking about what I would write about for my second book I knew that I wanted it to go beyond the snippets that you see online.

I wanted to talk honestly about money and what it's like to be the boss when you're working with your friends and family. All the things that you rarely hear social media entrepreneurs mention. In a world that can be a little tricky to navigate, our well-being is so important and there are some things I've learned in the last few years that can help us all live a bit more positively. I find there's nothing better for my mood than getting away, so I have also included guides to my favourite cities and shared all the places I love to visit for food, drinks, shopping and sightseeing.

But it wouldn't be a book from me without my other passions, so I'm also lifting the lid on my tips for renovating and designing a home, taking you through my wardrobe and beauty routine and revealing my not so secret passion for seasonal decoration and my beloved label maker!

It's three years since my first book and an awful lot has changed in that time. There's been a couple of houses, some new businesses, a second baby and an awful lot of fun! There's more to everyone than what we share online and I want you to see that, so sit down, relax and come with me – beyond Instagram.

Love Pippa x

PART ONE

Work

CHAPTER ONE

At Work

MY STORY

Some days, when I think of how far I've come, I have to pinch myself. I started out on this journey at a time of need. I was at home with a new baby, wasn't working for the first time in my career and I needed a plan.

People assume that I hit on an idea and had an overnight success on my hands, but, like a lot of businesses, my overnight success took six years of hard work! What was a simple blog and a Facebook page has grown into a website with over 150,000 views per month, a fashion brand, a lifestyle collection and a hugely successful events business. Sometimes when I'm asked if I'm a CEO I hesitate, but it's because with so much going on I'm often not sure what to call myself. At the end of the day I am a CEO and an MC and a designer and a wife and a mum and a friend and my own brand ambassador.

THE BEGINNING

I always relate things back to when Ollie was born. He's six now so that's basically how old Pippa.ie is. I started because I had no work, no money, and I needed to do something. I was bored. My modelling work had dried up when I was pregnant. There isn't much work for pregnant models in Ireland and I'd lost a big beauty campaign because I told them I was expecting, which was both shocking and disappointing. It wasn't a great time.

I knew that bookings would pick up again once I'd had the baby but I was really worried that I wouldn't be able to do it. Brian and I were living in Meath and we had no family nearby to help. Modelling jobs come in at very short notice and it was really difficult to organize things when I would get a call telling me I had to be in Limerick at 7am for a fashion show the next day. If Brian was working too, I had nowhere to drop the baby and no one to help.

I started posting outfit pictures on Facebook and they began getting more and more likes and comments. I realized that online might be the way forward, and maybe I should take it more seriously. A friend of mine helped me to put together a very basic WordPress website and I taught myself how to update it.

Ollie wasn't in crèche at that stage and it was all pretty easy to manage. I was posting pictures, writing short captions and maybe doing a Facebook post. Then my Facebook page started growing quickly and when I got near to 10,000 likes, I rang a hotel and asked them to give me a one-night stay as a prize for my first competition. They agreed and I ran the competition. Before I knew it, I reached 10,000 likes and I was absolutely delighted.

Then Pippa.ie started crashing and we didn't know why. At the time, Brian's production company were using a marketing company called iZest to build them a website. Brian casually mentioned the problem that we were having to Alan, who runs iZest, and he took a look for us. He quickly realized that it kept going down because the traffic to the site was insane, far too much for the little site I was running. We needed a new one. It was a big deal, and a really big investment at a time when we weren't making any money. We took a leap of faith and asked Alan and his team to build us a new site. We went from that free WordPress site at the beginning to now having Pippa.ie run on three servers. It's incredible.

Once the site was up and running I really wanted advertising on it, but I didn't know how to get it and no one seemed that interested. Our friend, Alan Clancy, owns some bars in Dublin, including 37 Dawson Street and House, and I asked him if I could put up a banner ad for 37. That was my first advertisement, a free ad for my friend's bar – but it worked!

Shortly after putting up the ad I got an email from a tea and coffee company asking if they could run a competition on Pippa.ie. They said they had a budget of €200. I couldn't believe that someone wanted to pay to advertise on my site, I jumped at the chance. No one was really doing those kinds of targeted ads or one-on-one brand collaborations on their websites at the time. Ollie was probably two by the time this all happened, so it wasn't fast, but it was a sign of things to come.

THE FASHION FACTORIES

We were ticking along with Pippa.ie, but I wasn't really making any money, we were struggling to pay the bills and I didn't know what to do next. Brian was working for RTÉ and people think that if you work in TV you're a millionaire. The reality is that unless you're in the UK or the US that's really not the case. Very few people in Ireland become millionaires from being on TV. Things were pretty difficult. I needed something to change.

I wanted to break away from modelling for good, for people to see me as something else, and I thought writing a column would help make that switch in people's minds. I emailed Jen Stevens, the editor of *U Magazine* at the time, and asked her if I could be a columnist – and she said yes! It was the first thing I did outside of working on the website at home, and the first thing that said Pippa.ie at the end of it. We were so excited and Mum bought every copy she saw.

By now I was getting inundated with messages to Pippa.ie asking me to do personal shopping. It didn't seem like the right fit for me, but I had so many requests I wondered if there might be something in it. It was actually Brian who suggested doing something with a group of women in a hotel, an evening thing that would be a bit of craic. It's the way Brian and I have always worked. We'll sit down and chat about what's going on, or a problem, or a potential idea – it's such a team effort.

Once we had the idea we just started running with it. I decided to sell fifty tickets to the first Fashion Factory evening event – it seemed like such a big number – and to do it in Powerscourt Hotel. Because it was the first one and I was so nervous, I probably over-compensated! The afternoon tea was outrageous and the goodie bag was insane. I gave everyone a complete brush set from Blank Canvas. It was too much but I wanted to make sure everyone had the best time. The costs were huge and I didn't make any money from it. At the time, I thought it would be a one-off, and I wasn't sure that I could take it anywhere. We met our friend David Webster, who was the manager of the hotel, after the event and he said, 'Pippa, you'll be doing it in the ballroom next!' I laughed. There was no way I was going to fill a ballroom and be able to stand up in front of a huge crowd – but that's exactly what we did a few months later.

It's crazy when I think of the start of Fashion Factories and how far we've come. If they were the only thing we did we would still be a successful business. They really have paved the way for everything we do. Which is probably why everyone was so surprised when we said we were taking a break from them this year. I'm not saying they're gone forever but things need to be changed up. I've been doing them successfully for four and a half years now and we held our last event in Limerick with 800 people.

We finished on a high, and now I want to move on to something new. I love being excited by things, having the spark of an idea and going with it, and that's what I'm doing now. I want to keep things fresh. I want to innovate. That's what keeps me going.

POCO

We launched my jeans range, POCO, in November 2016, but we worked on it solidly for a year and a half before that. When we began to work on it we really had no clue where to start. I knew what I wanted in my head, but I'm not a designer so we had to find a factory with an in-house designer that I could work with. But even finding that factory was a massive deal. No one wants to help you, people aren't very forthcoming with their contacts, and I totally get that.

As usual, Brian had someone who could help – honestly, he knows someone for everything! He had a friend who had been in the clothing industry and though they didn't specifically work in denim they were able to push us in the right direction. It was a vague direction though, sort of like telling someone to drive on the N7 to find St Stephen's Green, and we more or less had to work it out ourselves.

A lot of it rested on Brian's shoulders. I was pregnant with Louis and at the stage where I couldn't fly, so Brian was travelling to different factories, meeting manufacturers and FaceTiming me along the way.

There was so much research involved. We narrowed our fabric supplier down, and once we had that chosen and priced we moved on to the other costs – buttons, trims, rivets, not to mention shipping, taxes and customs,

there's so much involved. Even what kind of stitching you use makes such a difference to the bottom line. So much goes into the manufacture that you have to ensure all of those costs are in place before you even begin to think about how you're going to price your jeans.

When it came to forecasting and buying, my sister Susanna was a great help. We didn't know how many sizes to buy for our first order. I remember sitting in her kitchen, with the kids in the background, as she wrote down sizes six to sixteen – then we tried to figure out some numbers, '200 size tens, no that's not enough, 250 tens', '350 size twelves?' We were just guessing. I did have a little insight into what we might need though, as I was doing rewardStyle at the time, an affiliate shopping link system, and I could check on the back end of that how many jeans or jumpers of each size I had sold for different brands in the last two years. That was a big help as I had a rough idea of the sizes my followers were buying – but it was all still a gamble.

Before we had even told anyone about POCO our first factory order was for 8,000 pairs. I wanted to deal with the best factories and they all have a minimum order limit, which is terrifying. We used all our Fashion Factory money for it – and there was a good reason for this: we didn't have enough of a credit rating to get proper finance. I was still carrying a credit card bill from when we got married and it was through the roof. Which was, in hindsight, the best thing that ever happened to me, because I've never made that mistake since. I don't use a credit card now. We have a business one but that's it.

When we were almost ready to go we set up a POCO page on Instagram with a video that we'd made. We put up the teaser and announced that POCO was a new jeans collection – and the reaction was off the charts. We were so excited that Brian thought we should up our initial order. I thought he was joking. We hadn't sold a single pair at that point, but jeans have a pretty long turnaround time and the worst thing you can do is sell out and have no more for weeks. We had five styles and we thought we'd add a couple of hundred onto each style, but when you do that in sizes six to sixteen it quickly adds up. It seemed like a huge number, but thank God we did it, because otherwise we would have been out of stock straight away.

When we made the call to order more they thought we'd lost our minds. We were dealing with an English agent for the factory who was experienced in launching new brands internationally, so he had a good knowledge of the market. He advised us to 'go easy, I'd hate to see you left with 16,000 pairs of jeans', but we stuck to our guns and just went for it. Thankfully our instincts were right and they all sold out in a couple of weeks. It was mad.

THE PIPPA COLLECTION

Starting something new was another big risk and we all talked about it and mulled it over for a long time. I knew I wanted to do other things, but we didn't know whether to give that new thing its own identity or to put it under the POCO umbrella. We decided that, because POCO is so identifiable as a denim brand now, we should keep POCO as fashion only. We were thinking towards the future too and, not that this is going to happen any time soon, what would happen if we were to sell POCO on as a brand? Would we want everything to fall in under that or would we want to keep some of the business as a different brand?

Deciding what the next project would be was simple. Homeware has always been an interest of mine and it was an idea that I had been toying with way back at the beginning. I had grown up watching my mum decorate the house and it became ingrained in me. I still don't have any plans to launch a full homeware range, but I wouldn't be surprised at all if I did something like that down the line.

The candles and planners came out together – I decided on those two items for no other reason than they're two things that I really like. I found a really good fragrance house first and decided that we'd start with the candles'. That's the beauty of the Pippa Collection. It can be anything I want it to be.

Deciding to make a line of candles is one thing, actually knowing how to do it is a completely different ball game. The candle process was, to be honest, incredibly painful. Every single bit of the candle comes from a different place. We tested about thirty different wicks and discovered that some wicks don't

go with certain fragrances and they spit and blow up! Who knew?! I really wanted the candles poured in Ireland so trying to find someone to do that was a bit of a mission too. The beauty of having them poured here is that there's a quicker turnaround time, but you're importing every last element. We eventually found our candle vessel in Vietnam, the lids come from somewhere else, then there's the box – you're literally building a candle with parts from around the world.

I'm so happy with them, they're luxurious and a beautiful gift. They're available online and are exclusive to Brown Thomas. The first day I walked into the store on Grafton Street and saw them there I was an emotional wreck. I just stood there on my own crying and thinking how proud my mum would have been. People dream of having something they've made for sale in Brown Thomas – and I did it.

I've added to the collection this year with new fragrances, diffusers and at some point, I'd like to do hand cream to match the candle scents too.

Thankfully the diaries were a bit of an easier process. They were being printed in one place and I had full control over the design. I worked with a creative team on them and it was such a different experience because we were able to do it the way we wanted, with no outside elements dictating anything. They're sold out now and we might park them and think of something else stationery-wise. It's nice to be able to try new things and then change them up.

I've been very lucky that nothing we've done has ended up being a dud. I've been close to pushing the button on things and stopping them because I haven't had a good feeling about them. I'm probably a little too careful. We could be launching things way more often than we do. But literally everything we do is made from scratch for us, nothing is picked off a shelf, and that takes time. I don't want to make an expensive mistake.

I want to have integrity in what I do, so the things we sell cost money to make. I want to be faithful to who I am and think about what kind of consumer I am. What do I like? We don't have the Ali Baba business model where you buy things in bulk and put your name on them. No disrespect to anyone who operates like this, but it's just not something I would ever do. My tagline is 'affordable luxury' and I want everything we do to feel like that. It's a treat, it's a gift. They're something special to buy yourself, but they won't break the bank.

CHAPTER TWO

What I Know About Business

FINDING YOUR NICHE

Whether you're looking to launch what you hope will become your global empire or you're starting a side project that will bring you a little extra income, the first thing you need to do is find your niche.

Before I launched POCO, I had so many ideas going around in my head – and I still do – but the trick is being able to spot the one that will work.

Up until then I had been doing a lot of brand collaborations. I remember thinking, hmm, I'm selling all these things for other people and only seeing a small return. Then I got the opportunity with Blank Canvas Cosmetics to develop a make-up palette, the Pippa Palette, and sales exceeded expectations. I knew then that there might be a market for my own brand.

My first idea was to have a maternity line. When I was pregnant with Ollie I had been really disappointed with the clothes on offer and I was sure that a maternity line was a great idea. However, when we researched it we realized it wouldn't work for us. Women don't want to invest money in clothes they wear for such a short period of time.

I also wanted my own boutique. But, realistically, I wouldn't be able to be in the shop full-time and the overheads were too high for this to be a successful venture. Then I thought about establishing an online shop but Susanna, who worked for Nike, and Louise Kennedy, advised against this too: I'd be on buying trips constantly, I'd need updated stock all the time and I'd never be able to compete with the likes of ASOS. She told me to focus, and asked, 'Why are you trying to do fifty items of clothing? Why can't it just be one thing? What do you love wearing?' It was a light-bulb moment. I love jeans, I wear them all the time, people wear jeans in June and they wear them in December – they're seasonless. By the end of that conversation I was fired up. I knew I wanted my own denim brand and I was excited. I knew I had found my niche.

It would have been easy to give up when my first ideas weren't right, but that's what being an entrepreneur is all about. You have to keep coming up with things until you hit the one that's perfect for you.

How to find your niche

* Focus on what you're good at and what fits with your personal brand.

* Don't be afraid to come up with lots of ideas even if they don't work. You'll eventually hit on the right one.

* Do your research. Is anyone already doing your idea? You can't always reinvent the wheel, but sometimes you can do it better than everyone else.

* Have someone you can run your idea past. Make sure they're really honest!

* Figure out your funding.

* Take your time. It took me a year and a half to launch POCO. If it's going to be worth it in the long run, then take your time and do it right.

* Take the leap. Starting anything new is terrifying. But it's also brave and exciting. Go for it!

FACING YOUR FEARS

At my first few Fashion Factories, I felt sick to my stomach at the thought of getting up to speak in front of everyone. I'd bring loads of notes up with me and try to read through them on stage. I had no experience or training in MCing or public speaking. People always ask me if I've had coaching but I don't think there's any way of getting around it other than just getting up and doing it. I think you just have to feel the fear and do it anyway.

I wasn't great at the beginning, and I wasn't nearly as polished or confident as I am these days. Now I'm really relaxed and I can speak off the cuff, but, like anything, you have to start somewhere.

If fear is holding you back in your work then you need to take a deep breath and dive in. I could easily have said 'that's not for me' and it would have been the end of our events and essentially our business. It doesn't come naturally to me and I really had to push myself at the start.

If you're not being seen or heard in work because you don't like to speak up, or you're turning down the opportunity to present, you'll never get past that until you try.

How to stand up in front of a room

* *Fake it 'til you make it. Tell yourself you can do it. You'll trick your mind into believing that you can.*

* *Practise over and over again. Get a partner or good friend to be your audience and run through your presentation way more times than you think you need to. The presentation will work its way into your memory and you'll have to rely on your notes less.*

* *Make light of your nerves at the beginning of your presentation. People will warm to you and want you to do well.*

* *If it's really too terrifying, ask a colleague to do a joint presentation with you the first time. Twice the people is half the nerves!*

* *As with anything, the more you do it the easier it will get.*

BUILDING YOUR TEAM

One of the biggest responsibilities I faced was in building my team. We started slowly and everyone that's with us is an integral part of what we do.

Hiring the right people isn't always easy. First of all, I want people on my team who are excited about what I'm doing and share the same vision. When you respect people and look after them well you get that back tenfold. That's the approach I've always taken, and it's worked, and everyone with us genuinely would do whatever job is asked of them.

A lot of people will say that it's not a good idea to work with people you know well. Our team is a mix of family, old friends and new colleagues, and that works for us – but it may not work for everyone. Building the right team for you takes time so don't rush it. You want to be happy with who you have. You spend a lot of time with them and they're responsible for your success.

Niamh Doherty started with me as an intern five years ago. I was running the business from our house in Meath back then, so our first meeting was in Starbucks in Blanchardstown – the glamour! Niamh became my first full-time employee. She was only twenty-one when we met and it's been brilliant to see her confidence grow with everything we've done together. I hope it says a lot about me as a boss too, that she's still happily with us now.

My sister, Susanna, joined us next. She has great fashion industry experience and brilliant organizational skills. My friend of twenty years, Laura Treacy, came on board at first for Fashion Factory weekends and now she is an integral part of the team. She's also amazing at building flat-pack furniture! Laoise Moggan came to help us pack jeans at the start of POCO (we literally called her at midnight one night), but then I realized that she's a brilliant photographer and I nabbed her for the team.

Things to consider when building your team

*   *Start slowly.* *The temptation is there to have a head of this and a head of that but you want to take your time in putting your team together.*

*   *Think about people's personalities.* *Someone could be amazing at their job, but not be the right fit for your team. You all spend a lot of time together so the mix has to be right.*

*   *Get the right blend of skills.* *You need to make sure you have all key areas covered.*

*   *Work on your management style.* *It can be unsettling to start off as everyone's friend but as the business grows, you have to shut your door on them. Decide what type of boss you want to be early and try your best to stick to that.*

'When we moved into our new office I was a bit like, "Wow this is mad. That's my name up there. I have to pay all those people. I have two kids and a husband." It's so funny, I still don't think I'm old. I'm thirty-five this year and I still think I'm a young one.'

SKILLS

I'm a big believer in hiring people that have a specific, valuable skill. You can't cut corners and say 'Oh sure, how hard is marketing?' or 'How difficult is PR?'. It is hard and it is important. If you're not skilled or experienced in that area then find someone who is. Know the things that you're not good at and surround yourself with people who are. You'll reap the benefits in the long run. You don't have to hire people full-time. Work with them on a project basis if that's more cost-effective. Just don't try to be all things to all people, something will slip by you in the process.

Some of the areas I have outsourced

*   *Marketing. We're not a big enough company to have a dedicated in-house marketing team so working with an agency is perfect for us.*

*   *Fulfilment. At the beginning of POCO we were trying to do everything ourselves and that included packing orders at midnight. It was unsustainable and exhausting for everyone.*

*   *PR. I do a lot of our PR but when we have needed it for launches we hire someone like Tara O'Connor who is at the top of her game.*

BRANDING

You cannot overestimate the importance of branding, it sets the whole tone for everything before anyone has even seen what you're trying to sell. We had been trying to come up with a name for the line for ages and were going through all sorts of random ones. We all agreed we needed to simplify it and it turned out the answer was staring us in the face – my initials.

It's so simple, it's just four letters and it's easy to remember, exactly what you want in a brand. It still makes me laugh though that people don't realize POCO is Pippa O'Connor Ormond.

How to brand

* *Clearly identify yourself.* Consider the fonts you use, the colours, they all tell a story before people even know who you are so make sure they're representing you the right way.

* *Define your customer,* then design your branding to appeal to them. It makes no sense to do it the other way around. Think about what they would like.

* *Be creative in what you do.* Branding is about so much more than repeating your logo in different places. These days you need to think about the story you're telling on social media, on your website and on your packaging too. Become a creative storyteller and people will invest in your message.

* *Remember the radio test.* If a customer was to hear your brand mentioned on the radio and tried to find it, could they spell it easily? You don't want to create impediments to people finding you.

* *Be consistent.* People respond well to brands they feel they know, so if you start doing something outside your ordinary branding you run the risk of confusing your customer and them backing away.

FUTURE-PROOFING

An essential part of future-proofing your business is coming up with other projects that complement what you already have but offer a different revenue stream. With POCO up and running and the Fashion Factories working like clockwork, it was time to add something new into the mix. Most people would say sit back and enjoy what you have, but that's not the way my brain works – I'm always looking forward.

It's important in any business that you have other lines of income, so I would say to anyone – whether you have a big company, a smaller side project or are in the influencer space – to look for another complementary business to run alongside it. It's important to build your brand and then grow it and be responsible for your own revenue. Think ahead. What happens if my supplier goes bust? What happens if demand for my product or service starts to dwindle? If the worst happens, having a second line of revenue will keep you going while you regroup.

'You need to think of the bigger picture and not get bogged down in the nitty-gritty everyday running of the business.'

STRATEGY AND GROWTH

I'd say for a long time I was like a swan. If you'd looked in from the outside you'd have thought I was doing brilliantly. I totally looked like I had everything under control, but underneath I was swimming for dear life, trying to figure it all out. I learned pretty quickly that I couldn't strategize and grow the business if I was packing jeans. I wasn't able to think ahead. I couldn't see past the day I was in, and so we all quickly realized that I had to delegate. In business, you have to take chances, you have to get other people on board and that requires spending money, which is always very scary, but you have to take those risks in order to grow. Sometimes when I see businesses that aren't progressing it's because the boss is trying to do everything. In my experience if you try to do it all, not much of anything gets done.

If I'm sitting in the office all day every day, I'm not out meeting people, I'm not growing POCO, I'm not thinking of the next product. If I don't get on a plane and meet the factories and talk about trends, I'm not going to have new ideas, and we're not going to grow. I believe you need to think of the bigger picture and not get bogged down in the nitty-gritty everyday running of the business.

I have big strategic meetings with the whole team once every three or four weeks where we look at what's coming up. We work off a calendar and have things like Mother's Day and bank holidays marked off so we can plan for big events and weekends. You can't just be reactive to things, you have to be proactive and have a plan.

Sometimes things come along that you have no control over, like Brexit. We had to look at what we do in the UK and see what we could do if that becomes an issue. That's where the planning and the outside advice comes in useful. When you can see issues coming down the line you can fix them before they become major problems.

How to grow

* Sit with your senior team regularly and talk about where you are as a business.

* Discuss your competitors and see what they're doing and if you are still out-performing them. If so, how? If not, why?

* Have a marketing calendar and update it regularly. But don't be a slave to it. If you need to react to something quickly and move fast, don't worry that it's not on your calendar.

* Have six-month, twelve-month and five-year plans. Make sure there are targets that you are working towards and not only achieving but smashing.

* Get out. Travel, meet people, look at how your industry is behaving in other markets.

* Stay excited about what you're doing.

STRESS AND DELEGATION

When my mum died I realized that life is very short. Experiencing something like that is a shock to the system and it teaches you that, at the end of the day, it's only work. It's fine. Things might go wrong but no one is dying. That's the approach I have to it all. It's not the end of the world.

My worries would come from things at home more than at work. I'd like to say I don't feel guilty about leaving the boys, but sometimes I do. I'm getting better at it. I know that I'm luckier than most because our office is close to home so I can go back and forth a lot. I'm in and out. I'm always home by 4pm, that's a rule I have in my head and I stick to it. If you don't have self-imposed rules, you'll lose the run of things pretty easily.

I made a conscious decision to work like this, and I feel very lucky that I can. At the beginning, things were so busy that I didn't have the luxury of being at home as much. Now, because I'm confident in my team and I don't physically need to be sitting at my desk all day, I can pop out much more.

I'm the queen of delegation now, but I wasn't at the start. I ran myself ragged doing everything because I was trying to prove to the team that I was working just as hard as everyone else. But I've learned my lesson. It's okay to pass things over. People can do different jobs, everyone has different skills. I realized I didn't have to keep proving myself to anyone else.

I'm so good at delegating now that I have people who help me at work and at home. It's really important to say publicly that I have help at home with the boys. It frustrates me so much when you hear people say that they are just really good at managing things at work and at home when you know they have outside help: 'I'm just a good organizer' or 'I get up at 5am and do my work before the kids get up'. No. I've yet to meet anyone who does that in reality. Sometimes people are embarrassed to say that they have a childminder or a nanny or a cleaner. What are you embarrassed about? You're giving people employment and that's great. You're giving yourself less of a headache by not having to clean on your day off or at the weekend. If you're not scrubbing the bathroom, you have more time to spend with your kids. I don't see the problem.

Sometimes I think it's an Irish thing, that women are expected to do everything. We feel like we have to do it all. But we don't. If you have a partner, they can help, and if you have the means, you can get outside help. We don't need to be piling the guilt or the stress on ourselves.

Louis could be in crèche now but we have a nanny that minds him at home. He's just started preschool a couple of days a week to get used to it, but we have someone that we rely on heavily to help too. She's brilliant and has made our lives so much easier and everything functions better overall.

No one should look at my life, or anyone's life, and think I'm doing it all and feel bad about how they're getting on.

How to delegate

* *Ask yourself if you need to do it all.* Is your partner doing 50 per cent? Are you doing it all for an easy life?

* *Learn how to ask for help.* Don't wait until the situation blows up.

* *If you can afford it and want to – hire your help.* You're giving people employment and you're freeing up time to spend with your family.

* *As your kids grow up, give them jobs to do.* They'll become more well-rounded adults and you'll get more time in the bath!

* *Don't be a martyr.* Life is short, enjoy it.

'Mum used to laugh at me because when I was about seven or eight, I would plan my own birthday parties. I was always a bit funny like that. I'd go through the Golden Pages and ring up the balloon shop or I'd call up and organize a bouncy castle and casually say to Mum, 'Booked a bouncy castle'. I was always very independent. Mum and Dad separated when I was one. I grew up watching my mum work for herself. She was a Cordon Bleu chef and owned a catering company, and my dad was in the car business. Watching the two of them run their own businesses and seeing my mum work hard for herself was just normal to me and it obviously stuck. I like the idea of the boys growing up and seeing both of us work hard to achieve things for our family.'

My top ten business tips

1. *Have someone to bounce ideas off. Whether they are a formal mentor or a partner or friend whose opinion you really value, a sounding board is essential. No yes-men or -women allowed!*

2. *Be prepared to get your hands dirty at the beginning. You don't start off in a big glass office with a PA and a champagne fridge (actually, where's my champagne fridge?), it takes hard work and late nights. None of which you'll mind if it's something you're passionate about.*

3. *Learn how to delegate! Once you're up and running and there's money coming in, you have to learn how to delegate. Even if it's just one employee, learn how to hand them the jobs that don't need to be on your desk. Free up your time to strategize and grow.*

4. *Find people who have the skills you don't possess and hire them. If you're not brilliant with money, find an accountant, if marketing isn't your speciality, hire an agency. We're not all amazing at every single thing. If someone out there is better at something than you, get them on your team.*

5. *Take risks, nothing grows without them. It's terrifying, but if you keep playing things safe you may never make your millions.*

6. *Strategize: if you're not moving forward you're not moving. Research the big trends, see what your competitors are doing, stay at the top of your game and surprise people. If you don't, you'll stagnate, your customers will get bored, and you might even bore yourself – and that's a recipe for disaster.*

7. *Find your niche and do it well. What's the point in being the same as everyone else? Find the thing that makes you different and perfect it.*

8. *Future-proof your business and have alternative revenue streams. What if the single-stream business you have hits a wall, or a supplier lets you down or your manufacturer goes bust? An additional revenue stream works as insurance to protect your business if something goes wrong.*

9. *Live, breathe and eat your brand. If you don't know it inside out, who else will? Be your own brand ambassador.*

10. *Don't stress the small stuff, remember that it's only work. Seriously. Family, friends, your health and a little fun should all come before work. Life is short. Work to live, not the other way around.*

BUSINESS PODCASTS I LOVE

So Money by Farnoosh Torabi

Hosted by US TV presenter and author Farnoosh Torabi, *So Money* is a podcast that delves into the money strategies and success stories of top influencers, authors and business leaders. Guests include Tony Robbins, Arianna Huffington and Suze Orman among many others. You can hear about their philosophies, wins, habits and failures.

Second Life with Hillary Kerr

Hillary is the co-founder of Clique brands, which is the company behind successful website and clothing business Who, What, Wear. Hillary interviews people who have had a career change or pivot and talks about how they made the leap and how the traditional idea of one career for forty years is a little outdated. Hear from the likes of ban.dō boss Jen Gotch and actress turned businesswoman Jessica Alba.

WorkParty by Create and Cultivate

Create and Cultivate is essentially a female-focused business festival. Would-be female entrepreneurs gather to hear conversations about building businesses, raising money and marketing. *WorkParty* started life as a book by Create and Cultivate founder Jaclyn Johnson and now includes this excellent podcast and a new conference for millennial women.

Being Boss with Emily Thompson and Kathleen Shannon

If you have a side project that you've been trying to get off the ground, this is the podcast for you. Freelancers, creatives, part-time entrepreneurs, side hustlers, whatever you call yourself, this is where you can listen to interviews with some really interesting business people and hear how they deal with branding, marketing, business and how to put the systems in place that will help you to make money doing what you love!

Mothers of Invention with Mary Robinson and Maeve Higgins

This one isn't business based but we all need a little bit of inspiration in our lives and where better to get it than from a podcast fronted by comedian Maeve Higgins and former Irish President Mary Robinson. The two women, who first met when Maeve interviewed Mary for her podcast *Maeve in America*, are talking climate change. They say that the issue is a man-made problem with a feminist solution and meet a host of game-changing women fighting to save our planet.

Róisín Meets by Róisín Ingle

More inspiration and this time from *Irish Times* journalist and features editor Róisín Ingle. In each episode Róisín meets a fascinating person with an interesting tale to tell. There are stories of personal triumph and tragedy, there's music and there's usually a laugh along the way. This one is a great way to feel uplifted, empowered and educated – a great trio!

Owning It by Caroline Foran

Very few of us are a stranger to anxiety, and best-selling author Caroline Foran brings us a podcast that helps explain what anxiety is, why it happens, how our brains work and how to deal with it. It's a refreshing take on a difficult subject and each episode has personal experience and expert commentary to help you get through what you're feeling right now. Essential listening when you're overwhelmed by being a boss.

SEVEN IRISH BUSINESSWOMEN TO FOLLOW ON INSTAGRAM

1. *Ellen Kavanagh Jones @waxpertsellen*
   Ellen is the creator of award-winning waxing brand Waxperts, and each week she answers all your waxing- (and often life-) related questions during her Waxing Wednesdays Q&A session. You'll get glimpses into her life that include her super-cute son Cooper, her adorable dog and her hilarious husband Conrad.

2. *Jennifer Rock @theskinnerd*
   If you don't already follow Jen you need to immediately. She runs the brilliant skincare consultancy The Skin Nerd and is the founder of the Cleanse Off Mitt. Her Instagram combines brilliant skincare advice with her upbeat, inspiring take on life.

3. *Lucy Nagle @lucynaglestudio*
   Lucy's stunning eponymous cashmere label is one of my favourites and her fashion-business acumen is second to none. As well as being stocked in Brown Thomas, Lucy's pieces have been stocked in top-end boutiques around the world. Follow for a glimpse inside a luxury Irish fashion brand.

4. *Sonia Deasy @soniadeasy*
   As well as being the founder of award-winning skincare brand Pestle & Mortar, Sonia is a mother of five – how's that for multitasking?! Sonia's Instagram account is a window to her

international businesswoman life and is inspirational to anyone who dreams of creating their own brand. All that and Pestle & Mortar is based in Kildare – which you know I love!

5. *Oonagh O'Hagan @oonaghohag*
Oonagh is the MD of the Meaghers Pharmacy Group and is a powerhouse in the retail field. She has taken the business from a one-shop set-up to one with eight stores and a thriving online business. Oonagh is also a mum of two and knows all about the working-mum balance.

6. *Blanaid Johnson @cloud10beauty*
Blanaid is the CEO of Cloud 10 Beauty and is brilliant at getting exclusive beauty brands for Ireland. Her team are really creative, their social media is always innovative and fresh and I love working with her on our collaborations.

7. *Una Tynan @blankcanvascosmetics*
Una is the driving force behind Blank Canvas Cosmetics and she is a great example of how to run a business while personally remaining in the background. I love that Blank Canvas is a family-run business and that her right-hand woman is her sister Niamh, just like me and SuSu.

CHAPTER THREE

Social Media

I suppose I'd be lying if I said I wasn't always on social media. I have a Twitter account (@pipsypie), my own personal Instagram account (@pipsy_pie), one for POCO by Pippa (@pocobypippa), one for the Pippa Collection (@pippacollection) and the Pippa.ie Facebook page – and I have my eye on everything that goes on across these platforms.

The way I use social media has evolved over time though, and I probably share less now than I did a few years ago and that's for a few reasons – but mainly because I'm busier. Even though I'm in the public eye I consider myself quite a private person and I've always been careful about what I share. I don't like to put up every single detail of my life. It's important to have boundaries.

I go through phases and one day I might have loads of stories up on Instagram and another day I might not, but when I do they'll be about my lipstick or outfit or the office, it's not personal stuff really.

'As my husband says, being famous online is like being rich in monopoly, it's not real life!'

SOCIAL MEDIA AND THE BOYS

When it comes to the boys I'm changing how I do things, especially now that Ollie is getting older and is in school. He's aware of social media now and I'm very conscious of over-exposing the two of them. I'm fine with cute little snapshots, but I will never put up a post of them having a bad moment. It's not fair on them.

I'm also trying to be a bit more mindful of how much time I spend on my phone around the boys. Ollie has asked me to put it down so I can play with them a couple of times. Talk about feeling guilty. A six-year-old shouldn't have to tell you to do that!

I think, truth be told, that it happens to a lot of us now, not just to people who run online businesses. Social media has taken over our lives and although sometimes it's a lifeline if you're lonely, we probably need to be more mindful of how much time we spend aimlessly scrolling.

MY FOLLOWERS

Because Pippa.ie has been around so long, in online terms, I know a lot of my followers. So many have been there since the very beginning, which is so nice. I interact as much as I can and I get all sorts of messages, from 'what colour is your lipstick?' to much more serious matters like people asking for advice when their relationship is in trouble. I always try to reply to everyone, and when they're really serious ones I feel like I have to help.

Currently I probably get over a hundred DMs to my Instagram every day, which is pretty hard to manage. I had to turn the Facebook DMs off as I was getting too many to handle. The instant ones are still on Instagram, but even at that I still find it quite overwhelming.

I imagine people sometimes think there's a team monitoring my Instagram account, but no, it's just me! If you send me a message, it's me responding.

It is busy, but I'm incredibly grateful for all the followers who have helped grow the business. The best thing about it is that I recognize lots of the names from the last five years and I've met so many at Fashion Factories or at the POCO pop-up shops. I feel a huge responsibility to give people the time that they've given me over the years.

TROLLS

I think I'm incredibly lucky that, for the amount of people I have following me, I get trolled very little. You see some people online who get bashed every day and thankfully I have a miniscule amount of that. Some of that is because I'm not controversial and I don't say things to get a reaction; I'm not looking for attention so I don't think I'm giving people a reason to troll me.

There are definitely some people on social media who comment on things just to get attention, so how I deal with it really depends on my mood. If I'm feeling fierce I might write back to them, but I'm always pretty careful what I put down in writing. I say that to the team too – it's so important. Always be completely polite and respectful, even if someone is being rude or ridiculous.

But I very rarely respond. I won't delete but I won't engage, either.

THE INFLUENCERS

The term 'influencer' didn't exist when I first started out with Pippa.ie. It's funny, sometimes I sit back and I look around me; I'm in the middle of this industry but I often feel like I'm in my own little bubble and I don't feel part of it. When someone says 'Oh, you're an influencer', I don't feel like I am. It's hard to explain, but I think it's because I have all my businesses to concentrate on and I try not to get caught up with labels and terms.

PHOTOSHOP

Here's the truth about me and Photoshop – are you ready? I wouldn't have a clue where to start! I'll brighten and sharpen images on Instagram, the very basic bit that everyone does, but that's it. I'll always find nice light, but that's about the extent of it. Lili Forberg, who takes lots of my pictures for work and is an amazing photographer, despairs of me. She's always showing me great editing apps and tricks and then I don't use any of them!

People get really annoyed when images are Photoshopped, but altering images for ads, magazine covers and fashion spreads is not a new thing.

I do think the unrealistic images of female perfection on social media are tough for teenage girls – it puts a huge amount of pressure on them to look a certain way when there is so much going on in their lives already. I make a conscious effort to be as real and genuine as possible – life isn't perfect and neither am I!

SOCIAL MEDIA TIPS FOR STARTING OUT

Social media has been the foundation of everything I've done. Sometimes people say that I'm lucky because people knew me before I started the website, but that really could have gone two ways. They came out of curiosity at the beginning, but if it wasn't good, my audience wouldn't have stayed around.

Things online are different now. It would be so interesting to see how things would have unfolded for me if I was starting out these days. I had no money, so I had to be creative in coming up with ideas, events and businesses. Now posting sponsored content is a valid business model and possibly I would have been happy with that.

My advice to those starting out in social media now is not to just focus on today but to think long term and to have integrity. If someone is offering you money to promote something, ask yourself: would you wear that product or buy it yourself? If the answer is no then don't go near it. It's hard to turn down money but it's worth looking long term, and not at just one payment. People quickly see through anyone who flogs anything for a quick buck.

There should be integrity in advertising too. The rules in the UK and in Germany are much more stringent, which is the way it should be. People were, and probably still are, underhand about not disclosing if they've paid for an item, but it's also the responsibility of the brands, who often put people in a tricky position. They can be afraid to be seen paying someone to promote their product, when there's nothing wrong with collaborating. There's nothing wrong with making money – but it needs to be above board.

People still see the whole online influencing industry as a flash in the pan, but it's absolutely not going away. It's only going to get bigger. A lot of people have made huge careers from it. Look at Chiara Ferragni, the Blonde Salad blogger. She has over 16 million followers and is a great example of someone who has translated her blog into a huge business. And say what you want about the Kardashians, whether you love them or hate them, you can't deny the phenomenal empire they've built, underpinned by social media.

I think at the start of any industry people are sceptical. Digital business is still so new, but it's 100 per cent part of our media world now and will be for a long time in the future. I appreciate everything that my Facebook page and WordPress blog site have brought me, and it will be the way a lot of people start their businesses for a long time to come.

Social media tips

* Integrity is key – with what you post, how you present yourself, and who you work with.

* Be careful not to over-expose yourself – try to keep your private life as private as possible.

* Be honest – your followers need to trust you.

* Be careful what you share.

* Be tough and try not to react to or engage with negativity.

PART TWO

Home

CHAPTER FOUR

Interior Style

AT HOME

Between hosting Fashion Factories all over the country, travelling for POCO, running our pop-up shops and everything else that goes hand-in-hand with running Pippa.ie, I knew that I wanted our home to be a sanctuary for me, Brian and the boys.

We had moved house so often in the last few years – seriously do you know anyone who has moved six times?! – that I had lots and lots of ideas for what I wanted our forever home to look like. Brian and I love to entertain (more on that later!), so I knew the kitchen and dining areas had to be welcoming, free-flowing and elegantly casual to make our guests feel at home.

I really wanted the boys to have an area where they could just get on with being boys and all the toys and fun that entails. I also wanted proper chill-out zones for us as a couple. We don't get out on dates as much as we used to, so somewhere to unwind, have a drink and try not to talk about work or the boys was essential. And if that seems like a lot don't even get me started on what I had planned for upstairs!

A lot of what I wanted to do had been in my mind for years, but I picked up lots of tips from experts, designers and Instagram accounts along the way. You don't need to spend a fortune to have good design, you just need the right inspiration and some clever hacks!

COLOUR
YOUR WORLD

When it comes to a theme for a home I think it's really important to start with colour. Each room should be different but considered together they should still have a flow and complement each other.

I had Pinterest boards set up for all our rooms and colour was a big part of our design process. The colours we chose for every room are different, but essentially they're variations on a theme. They have the same undertone. We don't have everything in a soft grey and then one yellow room that completely jars. So, as you walk through the house there's a feeling of moving from one space to the next but without the overall aesthetic being interrupted.

Our more formal living room – the one we entertain in – is actually purple, but not a Barney the Dinosaur purple; it's a lovely soft colour with grey notes to it so that it blends in with the rest of the house. I've gone with the same colour on the ceiling too, which I think is a really modern and fresh take on design and you'll see a lot of it as you scroll through Pinterest. It can be a bit of a brave move and it only works if you have high ceilings and coving that you can paint in a contrasting colour to break it up a little.

When you're dealing with colour the best way to begin is to pick a focal point. In the living room I knew I wanted something a little different to grey on the walls so I started with the fabric I had found and loved for our couches and worked around that. I decided on the floors next, which I knew would be dark like the hall, and it all started to take shape from there. Funnily, the most frequently asked questions on my Instagram are what colour paint I have on the walls in the hall (it's Silver Moonlight by Colourtrend) and where we got our flooring (Design Emporium in Dublin)!

I did break my own design rule though, and I have one room of the house that's completely different to the others. Our guest bathroom downstairs is dark navy. I think people can be afraid of going for a really dark room but we've used a large mirror that bounces light from the window to give the illusion of more light. If you're going to take a risk with colour and do some experimenting, where better than the smallest room of the house!

Five ways with colour

1. Pinterest is your friend. Find interior design Instagram accounts that you love.

2. Think about tones for the whole house that will create a flow.

3. Begin with one thing, like a large piece of furniture, and work around that.

4. Get samples and swatches – you can never be too sure.

5. Remember that it's only paint, you can change it.

LUXURY IS IN THE DETAILS

I feel that the real personality of a room comes out in how you add details. Your finishing touches are as important as the big purchases you make – but they don't all have to be expensive. We've all been in rooms that feel empty and devoid of personality, and if you look around it's because they're missing the little personal touches.

I take a real high-low approach to all my decorating. I have pieces that belonged to my mum, Louise, all around the house, then I have some good pieces that I've invested in from interior stores (interior shopping really is my new addiction) and then I'm a big fan of mixing in things from HomeSense and TK Maxx because you can find incredible things there.

BLOOMING GORGEOUS

One of the most important decorating tools for me is flowers. I love to have the house full of them, but I do a mix of beautiful fresh bouquets and silk flowers. I love the real thing at home, but they're not always convenient to get, not to mention expensive. If I am buying fresh I'll go to M&S, their flowers just seem to last forever, and Appassionata in Dublin is my absolute favourite florist for when I'm going all out and want something special.

I have also invested in some premium silk flowers. I have a big multi-stem orchid on the island in the kitchen that people always think is real, and calla lilies in the other rooms. When it comes to silk flowers you really need to buy the best you can afford. They'll seem expensive at the time but they'll last for years and years. I've gone with one colour palette for the silk flowers and that way they can be mixed around, but they look great even up against the fresh bouquets and that's exactly what you want.

> 'I love tulips in the spring and eucalyptus is such a lovely economical way to decorate – it smells gorgeous too. But my absolute favourite are hydrangeas, they remind me of my mum and I had them at my wedding. They'll always be really special for me.'

TRAY CHIC

My other trick for accessorizing a room is to use lots of trays. I have them in different sizes and I make really nice set-ups on them which then can be moved around the room or out of the room depending on the season. They might have a bell jar with a candle, a book and an ornament for a side table. Our coffee table has a larger one with a really stunning Culti diffuser and my favourite coffee-table books on it, and the trays on the bookshelves have smaller set-ups. Inevitably, almost every tray will feature candles!

I've always got my eye out for different sizes and types of trays and have wooden ones, gold and silver ones and beautiful mirrored ones. The trays are a great way of refreshing a room, and when the space feels like it needs a bit of a change I can move things around easily. After Christmas, I just wanted everything be quite minimalist again, so when all the decorations were gone I just swapped out some of the trays on the shelves and pared everything back. It felt like a completely new look for the room and it took no time at all.

'When I'm styling my trays I use pieces of different heights to add interest; look out for quirky objects to mix in with candles, books and flowers.'

BURNING LOVE

Of course, candles play a huge part in my home – how could they not when I have my own range? I have Pippa Collection candles everywhere, which I love, but I do like a mix of heights and designs, so there are also lots of tealights, tapered candles and pillar candles in each room.

I love putting big pillar candles into vases and I think it's a great inexpensive way of creating a focal point. I like one scent in each room, so I would light something like the Pippa Collection Sultry Privé candle, and then keep all the accent tealights and pillar candles unscented. I like to use different scents in different rooms to create a mood – our Pippa Collection Mandarin and Mint candle is so good in a kitchen, though I would use unscented candles for the table where you're eating.

I'm a great bargain shopper so I love picking up candles in TK Maxx or IKEA, I think they're incredible for the price. When it comes to scented candles and diffusers I often pay more for quality – they smell better, and last longer.

THROUGH THE LOOKING GLASS

Finally, when it comes to details I think you can't overestimate the usefulness of mirrors. They're amazing for adding light and interest. I've used them as a design feature in every house we've lived in over the years. I think mirrors are the cheapest way to bounce and create light and to make the space feel bigger.

It's not about being able to see yourself in every room – you can't even see into lots of the ones we have in our house because they're up too high – but without them a corner would seem darker and part of the room would feel smaller. I'm all about maximizing the light. After all, we live in Ireland and a house has to work at 4pm in December as well as at midday in July. I absolutely love fires and cosiness in the winter, but if I can get a little more natural light into a room, I will.

Get the look

* *Finishing touches add personality.*

* *Use trays to create vignettes and swap them around whenever you're bored with a room.*

* *Flowers, flowers and more flowers. Invest in good silk ones for the weeks you don't pick some up with the shopping – just remember to dust them.*

* *Go with one scent per room then add lots of tealights for twinkly gorgeousness.*

* *Mirrors create light and space.*

* *Don't overspend on all your little bits and pieces, bargains can make you happy and look beautiful.*

BEFORE FOREVER

We've lived in six rented houses. Looking back, I don't know how we moved so many times, though I will say I'm an expert packer now. One of the things I got really good at was making a rented space seem like our home. It doesn't take too much to change the feeling of a house and it's something you really want to do to make it yours.

Painting a house goes a long way and landlords are usually delighted if you offer to do it yourself. Go with a neutral colour to keep the landlord happy and to keep it feeling fresh and then use all your favourite bits to accessorize.

I never spent lots on the things I used to decorate our rented homes because I knew they might not necessarily go with the décor in the home we would eventually buy, so it was M&S and TK Maxx cushions in the living room. I never wanted to spend money on getting carpets cleaned or changed because they weren't ours, so big rugs from IKEA to cover any ugly floors were ideal. Then I'd add my family pictures, candles and even the odd lamp to make it feel more like my own home.

Moving so many times did make me better at streamlining – I was using the Marie Kondo method before we knew who she was! I'm so different now to how I was five years ago. I would have kept everything then, but I think I'm less sentimental now. I keep the right things but not everything just for the sake of it. If it doesn't serve a purpose I'm a big believer in getting rid of it. Does it spark joy? No? Bye-bye!

Make a house a home

* *Ask if you're allowed to paint, most landlords will be thrilled.*

* *Rugs, cushions and throws cover most ugly sins.*

* *Add the things that make you happy like books, candles and personal pictures.*

* *Don't spend too much money if you're only buying to suit that house, chances are you won't be keeping them long term.*

KIDS' SPACE

I've learned a lot from every house I've lived in but one of my biggest lessons came with the arrival of Mr Ollie Ormond. The dynamic of your house changes dramatically when kids enter your lives, and everyone has to learn to adapt!

TOY STORY

Children come with a lot of things – no surprise to any mum or dad reading this – and I did it all wrong. I thought the best thing to do was to dedicate a room to it all and I just kept filling that room. Two houses ago I was looking at how we were using the space and I thought that the dining room, which we very rarely used, was just a waste. So I turned it into a playroom and filled it with toys. It only ever worked if it was pristine because although it was a decent-sized room there was so, so much in it. I don't mind admitting that it was a bombsite. Sometimes I think the more space you have the worse it is because you just fill it.

What have I learned over the past six years? Well, kids don't need that many toys, really they don't, and they definitely don't need a whole room dedicated to them. At certain points in the year, like before birthdays or Christmas, you should do a big clear out, go through everything and ask yourself 'Have they outgrown that?'

Sometimes it's you being sentimental and holding on to things, not your child. You need to really look at things and ask yourself if they can go to a friend's child or to charity.

I also learned some important lessons about storage. I had things up too high in other houses, which means that firstly the kids can't see them so are less likely to play with them and if they do know the toys are there you constantly have to help get things down for them, which is infuriating for

them and pretty annoying for you. All the kids' storage is low down now so it's all on their level and they can help themselves. I have big, deep, pull-out drawers and at the end of the day it's easy for everything to be thrown back in. I will say though, if you're renovating or doing a new-build, look out for the soft-close drawers – with children around you really don't want anything they can slam!

I know that not everyone has got the space for a separate playroom – I didn't in some of my previous homes – but I think we can all be a little bit clever with how we divide space. In a previous house we had a console table behind the couch to divide the room. We made the area behind the table the toy area and that really works. It's a clever space solution.

When it comes to tidying up, I make it into a kind of a game. If you have children who have been in crèche you probably already know the clean-up song, which we sing in the evenings and try to make the place tidy before bed. We do that downstairs and in their room too. We have Billy bookcases from IKEA in their room that hold loads and I have some buckets with stuff in them as well.

'Yes, it can be painful and emotional to go through your child's toys and get rid of stuff but you'll be glad of it at the end of the day. Take a few hours and be honest and ruthless. The decluttering will be good for your home and for your mind in the long run.'

SHARING IS CARING

When we moved into this house, we decided that the boys would share a room. We didn't know how it would go or if it would last that long, but honestly, it's been great. They're such little pals and hearing them playing and chatting in their room is lovely.

We bought them bunk beds, which I knew they'd love. The ones they have are from Harvey Norman and they're great. They have a pull-out drawer underneath for more storage. They're really sturdy, and they have steps up to them, not a ladder, so it's not too steep.

They have a bookcase on the back, which is so good for all their little bits. Ollie has a lamp on his shelf and all his writing things. He's learning to write at school now and he keeps writing little notes and letters at night-time. We find little pieces of paper with 'Mama' and 'Ollie' and 'dog' on them. It's very sweet.

The other thing I've implemented in their room is that they have their own washing basket. I think you need to start that kind of thing early on. They know that if things are dirty they go in there, I don't even have to say it to them anymore.

'If you are thinking of making your little ones share I'd say go for it. The first few weeks might be a learning curve and you may find yourself sitting outside their door listening as they run riot, but hopefully, like my two, they'll settle into it and it will be the cutest thing you've ever done.'

CHAPTER FIVE

In the Kitchen

GRAND DESIGNS

The kitchen is the heart of the home – and it's important that it suits your needs.

If you are thinking about getting a new kitchen, my advice is to list out all the things you want and see if and how you can fit them into your space.

Here's what was on my list:

* *A larder press*

* *Hidden bins*

* *Tray drawers*

* *A boiling tap*

* *A built-in cutlery tray*

* *Deep drawers*

* *A clear island*

* *A sink with a view*

* *A built-in kitchen table*

It's quite a list, isn't it? But all of those things are space savers or have a purpose. Let me explain.

I love our larder press. It's about the same size as an American fridge-freezer and it means that all your food items are in the one place. Between it and the fridge, there's no food anywhere else in the kitchen, which means it's easy to keep track of what you have, the rest of the kitchen presses are freed up for other storage and you only have to drag the shopping to one area of the room!

I try to keep it as tidy as possible, so our pastas and cereals are all decanted into clear airtight containers that keep everything fresh and make sure that no one puts an empty box back in. I pick up storage containers in M&S and HomeSense and I get Mason jars whenever I see them in TK Maxx, they're so useful. I'm also the type of person that buys a tin of biscuits because I like the tin, so there are plenty of those around!

Hidden bins are a game changer. Seriously. You may think I'm being dramatic, but not having a bin (or three) on show after years of having plastic bags hanging off doors is so nice. I have a regular bin, green bin and brown bin in a large pull-out drawer. There's also a secret pull-out tray above the bins where I keep the black, green and compostable bags and it's a big help in keeping everything in its place.

To streamline the countertops even more we have a boiling tap. It's easy to use, provides instant boiling water and also has a filtered cold-water function. It means there's no kettle on the counter which, as a very dedicated tea drinker, I took a little time to get used to, but I love it now.

I've had cutlery drawers with a cutlery tray that was slightly too small in most of my houses. It's always a dirt trap, there's never enough room and things always get stuck underneath. If you can get one built into the drawer or get one to fit perfectly – do it. It seems like an unnecessary thing to focus on but think about the amount of times you've looked down into your cutlery drawer and thought 'ugh'. A built-in one is still going to get dirty but not nearly as disgusting as what we've had before.

I feel like my deep drawers are such a revelation. There's no getting down on my knees to find a pot hidden at the back of a low shelf, there are no useless corner presses. You just pull them the whole way out and see everything you own. A simple but brilliant hack.

A sink with a view is probably very self-explanatory but if I really have to wash dishes I'd like something nice to look at!

I love my island so much. A lot of the pictures I looked at on Pinterest had islands with either the hob or the sink on them but this was one design feature I was sure of from the start. I wanted mine to be completely clear. Sometimes Brian and I eat at it, sometimes the girls and I have a drink at it. It can be a work space. If we have guests it's a great place to put canapes. A big bunch of flowers in the middle of it makes it a focal point. Basically, by keeping it clear it's versatile.

The built-in table was 100 per cent done with the boys in mind. It's easy for them to reach and it's where we all have our meals, and where Ollie does his homework. It's a great family space. It's practical too, as the seats are covered in a wipeable fabric – essential with two little monkeys.

LITTLE HANDS

I don't have child locks on any of the presses in the kitchen, I never have. The boys just don't go through the presses, they've never been interested. We have gorgeous velvet chairs at the dining table too and they haven't put sticky hands on them either. I did put their treats at their level in the larder press though, which might turn out to be a really bad decision because they know exactly where they are! My advice is to just encourage kids to learn what they can and can't do in the kitchen from the outset – whether for safety or aesthetic reasons. If they listen, of course!

LIGHT AND BRIGHT

The kitchen is white and I do get asked a lot about its practicality. The last few kitchens we had were very dark and I just couldn't wait to get a nice, bright kitchen. I think people are put off having light surfaces but you're going to have to wipe your countertops regardless, aren't you? Also, when it comes to a lighter floor I went for big tiles, because I've had small tiles before and all the food and dirt gets into the grout grooves. The big tiles are much easier to keep clean even though they're light.

KEEPING THINGS CLEAN

What are my cleaning tips? Get a cleaner, ha! I'm no Mrs Hinch but my mantra is 'little and often'. I have friends who spend the whole day Sunday cleaning the house and I get it, if you're busy or out working it might be the only time you have, but I prefer ten or fifteen minutes every day. That way I think you can keep on top of things and it doesn't all pile up.

'Speaking of cleaners, I know people who are incredibly busy and say "Oh I feel bad that I have to get a cleaner". No, you work, you have kids, you're busy, you deserve to have a cleaner come in once a fortnight. It's money well spent.'

COOKING LIKE DELIA

You'd swear I was the first person in the world to get a slow cooker, but I love it. It's amazing because I'm so busy, but in the morning I can just throw something in there and get on with the day and eight hours later there's a dinner, done.

THE ENGINE ROOM

In this house, we were lucky to have the space for a utility room, but I think if you can hide away your machines – whether that's in a garage or behind a set of double doors so it looks like a larder press with some shelves or a rail above – it's great. There are so many brilliant suggestions for tiny laundry rooms on Pinterest you'll get carried away pinning. I keep all our cleaning stuff in ours, and to be honest it can become a dumping ground.

CHAPTER SIX

Decorating for Seasons

When Susanna, Cian and I were growing up, my mum would have the house decked out for every occasion. When literally no one was decorating for Easter my mum had it all – little nests with eggs and decorations around the house. She always had branches or trees for every occasion. There'd be an Easter tree, a Halloween tree, an everything tree, so to me it was completely normal. It's only in recent years that everyone started doing it.

I love my house to feel cosy and homely, and that's definitely something I got from my mum. I really enjoy collecting all the decorations. I always decorated for every season, but the collection has really grown since the boys came along. Now that we're in our forever home I don't mind investing in decorations that bit more, because I know that I'm going to have them for years. I'm investing in memories.

TRICK OR TREAT

For me, Halloween is nearly as big as Christmas. Years ago, you couldn't get any decent themed decorations that weren't Christmas related, but now you really can.

I'm doing it for the boys but I'm doing it for myself too. Last Halloween I got these really lovely white ceramic pumpkins and Ollie was asking if he could paint them and I had to explain that they weren't the type for painting! They're Mummy's pumpkins. I probably am doing a lot of the decoration for myself because I'm the only woman in the house – it's nice to do the nice things. Even though Ollie's only six, if I ask him 'What does Mama like?' he'll say 'Candles, decorating, flowers!' So even he knows what I like.

I also bought little pumpkins that the kids can paint. They're really cute and only cost a few euros but they make a lovely rainy afternoon activity. Then when they're done I like to write their name on the bottom or the back and the date. To me that's how you make family memories and traditions, and those things are really important to me. Imagine taking those out in years to come or being able to give them to the boys when they're adults – things they made when they were five and two.

We have a long console table in the hall and I like to make that a seasonal focal point so for Halloween my grown-up pumpkins will take centre stage with foliage.

I like the front of the house to be done too, so I have a wreath for every season and I add things like big pumpkins and lanterns for Halloween.

EASTER PARADE

Decorating for Easter is the latest trend and I embrace it, of course. I always go in advance to see what's around the shops for seasonal decorating because the good things sell out really quickly. I start getting Easter things at the end of January. I recently bought some lovely things in The Range, which is a great place for arts and crafts bits.

In terms of decorating, I do all the mantelpieces and I add things to the trays I have on the tables and shelves. I decorate the console table and will always have a festive Easter wreath on the front door.

JINGLE BELLS

Christmas is my favourite time of year, it always has been.

We have a couple of trees so that I can decorate one and the boys can do another. If you're getting an artificial tree – and that's what I have – you should spend what you can absolutely afford on it, because you'll have the tree for years and years. Up until this year I was using my mum's tree that she bought about fifteen years ago. It was €250 at the time and I remember thinking it was a fortune, but we really got the years out of it. It was beautiful.

I have collected decorations over the years. I have ones the boys have made, ones from the different countries we've visited and family ones. I fill it out with bigger, cheaper baubles and then use my hero ones where you see them.

We have a smaller kids' tree and Ollie decorated it himself last year. I just left him to it and he loved it. Half the decorations ended up on the ground and that was fine because it was where he wanted them. I have my tree and they have theirs.

'When it comes to Christmas lights, more is more! You need good lights and personally I like warm white. I think it's the cosiest, the most luxurious looking.'

I wrap fake presents to put under the tree. I use shoe boxes. I don't put any real presents out until Christmas Eve so the fake ones really add to the overall look and it doesn't matter if the boys open them because they're just boxes.

When Santa comes to our house he doesn't wrap presents – he's just too busy! I put the presents in these lovely burlap sacks. You can get personalized ones everywhere now and they look so good.

The rest of the house doesn't get left out at Christmas either. If there's a space, it gets decorated. Cushions get changed, there are Christmas candles (our Warming Winter Pine is particularly good for this time of year) – but I draw the line at festive toilet seats! We have garlands everywhere and wreaths too. We have a new front door, so next year I plan to have a gorgeous wreath and bay trees decorated for Christmas and lanterns and candles – the festive works.

The perfect tree

* *Buy the best you can.*

* *Measure your space, you need to make sure it fits.*

* *Remember the stand and a nice stand cover.*

* *Pick a colour theme you love, you'll have your decorations for years.*

* *Make fake presents to put underneath to add that extra festive touch.*

STORAGE WARS

The hardest part is putting it all away again but I'm getting better at it. I've made so many mistakes over the years in firing decorations haphazardly into bags so I didn't know what I had.

I'll only put things into clear boxes now and use my label maker to mark them. Everyone needs a label maker! I've had so many houses and so many years of not doing it right that now I really make an effort. It doesn't come naturally to me, I make myself do it.

Christmas storage is especially important because there's so much to pack up. This year I bought big clear boxes in HomeSense and I packed everything tree by tree, room by room. I took down the lights properly, wrapped them up and put them into sandwich bags. Then I put each sandwich bag of lights at the bottom of the boxes and all the decorations for the tree went in on top of them. Then you have a whole tree done in a box, ready for next year. It just makes things so much easier. You'll be thanking yourself the next year for being so organized!

'There were years of putting decorations into black sacks and old shopping bags and then shoving them into the back of the attic. I would have no idea what was in there. I'd only find stuff when I moved house two years later.'

CHAPTER SEVEN

Entertaining at Home

HOUSE PARTY

Brian and I love entertaining. Having people over is one of our favourite things to do. I'm not the greatest cook in the world, so I'm always thinking of ways around that.

I'll have people over at a certain time so it's just drinks and canapés, which I can handle. I personally prefer a relaxed atmosphere and good music. I'm a believer in not killing yourself. If you're an amazing cook and entertainer, brilliant. If you're not, you should enjoy yourself too, without the stress.

Even if you're just serving drinks you have to be organized. You have your best glasses out and clean, and your wine, prosecco or champagne on ice. Everything takes time and effort. The only problem with drinks and canapés is that our parties don't tend to end. Lots of times we've ended up ordering a takeaway for everyone.

My skill is making people feel welcome and handing them a glass of something delicious. The house looks good, there are candles everywhere and we have great music. I have lots of playlists on Spotify for different occasions. The people, the atmosphere, the drinks and the music are what I like to focus on.

'I'm a good reheater and I'm great at serving a drink.'

JUST THE TWO OF US

I take the same approach to a drinks night if it's just me and Brian. We don't get to go out as much as we used to and sometimes it's far too easy to fall into the trap of lying on the couch, turning on the TV and staring at your phone. Now, don't get me wrong, we do that too, but sometimes I try and make a drinks night just for us. I'll set up a tray and I'll put glasses out, some little snacks in a bowl and set the scene. Then I'll light candles and lamps for a bit of ambience, and we'll be all set up. We try to limit work talk and make it feel like we've gone out for a date, even though we're at home.

'Brian makes such a good G&T that, even if you didn't like them before, you'll definitely like them after one of his.'

PART THREE

Fashion

CHAPTER EIGHT

In My Wardrobe

Fashion and what I wear is a huge part of what I do. From the very beginning it has been the backbone of Pippa.ie and when I transitioned to having a fashion business of my own with POCO it became even more important. But it probably wasn't until I was in my thirties, until I had Ollie I suppose, that I felt really comfortable with my own personal style. Before, I was always conscious of wondering 'what will people think' or 'what should I be wearing' or 'what's on trend' instead of just going with my gut.

Nowadays I just wear what I like – and while I do keep an eye on trends and like to know what's going on, I'm much better at choosing what I know suits me or fits in with my style. I absolutely adore fashion but now I make it work for me instead of the other way around.

My style has definitely pared back over the years. Where in the past I would have had everything going on – the tan, the hair, the big earrings – now I'm more restrained. That's partly age, but it's mainly understanding what works for me. And it's something that's not too difficult to learn.

If there are routinely pictures of you where you aren't happy with the way you look, ask yourself if it's because of what you're wearing. Maybe big chunky jumpers don't suit your shape or maybe your turtlenecks would be better swapped for V-necks. Should those on-trend midi dresses be taken up two inches to elongate your legs, or should you be wearing more colour around your face?

Learning what really suits you can save you time and money. If you're not confident in seeing what that is then get a sister or good friend around to your house, try on lots of different shapes and styles and get them to snap a picture of you in them. Then look at the pictures and be brutally honest. It might take a couple of hours but at the end of the day you'll know what's working and what isn't. It may seem boring to some, but having a personal style that you stick to makes shopping much easier, and you can always play with pattern and texture within the shapes that work for you.

Because fashion really is my business my wardrobe can get a little out of control but I've developed ways of managing it over the years.

THE RAIL TRAIL

First up is my rail. I think everyone should have some sort of freestanding rail. I know it's not always appropriate space-wise, but it doesn't have to take up too much room and it's going to save you a lot of time and heartbreak. I use it for planning and getting organized, and whether you're heading off for a few days of work travel or going to the office every morning, having everything sorted on your rail before you start the week is such a lifesaver.

I take things out of the wardrobe, hang them up and then accessorise them so I know what bag I'm going to use, which shoes and earrings. Then I know what I'm wearing every day. I would generally do it on a Sunday or before I pack for a trip, and it means that I don't bring more than I need because I can see it all in front of me before it goes into the bag. Before, I always threw extra 'just in case' outfits into the bag and would end up more confused than ever when I got to my hotel.

I find the whole thing quite therapeutic and relaxing. The boys go to bed and I head to my rail. I use velvet hangers for a bit of luxury – I got mine in TK Maxx – and I start planning my outfits. It might sound silly but then I can go to bed feeling more organized and ready for the week.

> 'We all have things that we haven't worn or used properly and it's a waste. I think planning like this is like shopping in your own wardrobe. You'll find things you forgot you had!'

FOLDING, HANGING AND CLEARING OUT

THE BIG CLEAR-OUT

How you store your clothes is so important to how they last and how you see them. Having things stacked on top of each other really hinders your ability to see what you have, but one of the biggest impediments to proper storage is keeping things for far too long.

I used to do a big clear-out once a year, but now I try and do it as I go. It's much less overwhelming and, because I know it's not going to be a huge job, I tend not to put it off. If I keep pulling something out of my wardrobe, looking at it and putting it back in, I now try to figure out what's wrong.

If I don't like it, it doesn't fit or doesn't suit me – it's gone. I do different levels of clear-out. If it's worn to bits and no good to anyone it goes to fabric recycling. If something is nice but I'm realistically not going to wear it again I'll ask one of the girls if they want it, especially if they're looking for something to wear to a wedding or an event. Then everything else goes to the charity shop.

What you're left with is a wardrobe full of pieces you like and which make you feel good; pieces you'll wear, clothes that suit you. I find that it's a great way of mentally logging what you have so you don't keep buying the same thing over and over again.

BIKINI BUM NOTE

Another area I recently began clearing out is holiday wear. I think everyone has that holiday bag or box of things that they take out once or twice a year for the sun. They are usually cheaper clothes that don't make you feel good and you wonder 'Why am I hanging on to these?' We're all guilty of going shopping each year, buying cheaper things and then getting to your destination and realizing everyone is wearing the same things as you!

Now I try to buy one or two nicer things each year and put them away for holidays. A beautiful kaftan or a quality bikini that you'll have for years can really add to your holiday basics. If it's important to you to look good for fifty weeks of the year, you shouldn't feel terrible for those two weeks by the pool. Sitting around in front of strangers in less clothes than usual comes with lots of hang-ups already, so we should be doing everything we can to feel better, not worse, about ourselves.

People always talk about rotating your wardrobe for the season and I don't really do that. I'll keep the high summer things separate – I'm not likely to wear a kaftan around Kildare – but Ireland's weather being how it is, you need access to jumpers in July and shorts in September. It's a big commitment to pull everything out each season and vacuum pack it and put it away. If it's something you need to do for space then of course you have to do what works, but maybe see if there's a way of organizing your wardrobe without hiding half of it.

STORAGE SOLUTIONS

I like to store things where I can see them so I keep my shoes out and on shelves. I have built-in ones in my house now, but previously I used Billy bookcases from IKEA and they looked great. I found that if I kept my shoes in their boxes I never wore them – out of sight is out of mind. Yes, this way means I do have to take them off the shelf and dust them every so often but that's a commitment I'm willing to make to my shoes (we have a very good relationship)!

I use the velvet hangers in my wardrobe too. They look good but they're also very practical: things don't slip off them, they're incredibly slimline so you can fit more in and it makes you feel like you're being nice to your clothes, you know? Like you're treating them well.

I fold things like chunky knits both because of space and because if they're heavy they can stretch badly when hung. When I'm folding things like t-shirts I'm careful that they don't go into really deep drawers where you can't see them. It's sort of like the Marie Kondo way of storing things. Maybe I'll call it Pippa Kondo. She is right about being able to see what you have. Layers and layers of things folded and put in on top of each other in deep drawers means that you'll quickly lose track of what you have.

I'm also very careful with how I store jewellery. Things you love can get tarnished or broken so easily when they're all just fired in together. My favourite way of storing them is in a shallow drawer with dividers. That way necklaces and earrings lie flat, there is less chance of them being broken and it's easier to see what you have. Do I sound like a broken record yet? Seeing what you have is the key to a great wardrobe. Fewer things, stored with care and so you can see everything, means you'll wear them all more often.

WEAR YOUR BEST.
EVERY DAY.

I'm a big believer in not keeping things for 'special occasions'. Seriously, what are you waiting for? People will say 'Oh I have a great coat that I keep for weddings' and I think, why would you do that? If it's gorgeous and you love it, wear it all the time – wear it to weddings, but wear it with jeans and trainers during the week. Otherwise what's the point of making that investment? It's not an investment if you wear it three times a year. It's like your good candles or your good sheets. Make yourself happy, wear the clothes, burn the candles, sleep on the sheets. Be good to yourself.

> 'My biggest tip when it comes to your clothes is to get a steamer. I hate ironing almost as much as I hate washing clothes and a hand-held steamer is a game changer. It's quick, easy and you'll never really have to iron again! I bet if you get one you'll be straight onto me to thank me for the tip! I've even heard of people steaming their sheets on the bed.'

COST PER WEAR – MY KIND OF MATHS

We all have to think more about how much we're buying. We have a responsibility to think about the sustainability of fashion and the environment. I'm trying to spend more wisely and get things that I actually really want and will look good for longer. It can be hard in my job not to buy new things all the time, and I do love an online purchase, but I think if I wasn't working so much and on stage all the time I wouldn't buy as much.

Now that I know what I like and what suits me, I like to really invest in those pieces. For me, that's things like good-quality cashmere (if you look after cashmere you'll have it for years and years), a good leather jacket, flat leather boots that you wear every day – and jeans, of course.

My black leather jacket is from Maje and it just keeps getting better. The more you wear it the softer it becomes and the nicer it looks. I kept buying faux leather jackets in different colours, like orange or red, that I would wear only a few times. Eventually I thought no, I should just buy one good one that I'll have for a long time. I'm really glad I invested in it. I wear it all the time and now it's one of my staples.

I get some of my cashmere from Irish brand Lucy Nagle, which makes really beautiful pieces. I wear and wear my cashmere, like I really use them, they're definitely not just for good wear. I also invest in good tailored pieces. I love a good blazer. They look as good with jeans and heels for an event as they do with a tee and trainers for the school pick-up or at the weekend when you want to feel put together with minimum effort. And who doesn't want that?!

SPECIAL OCCASION INVESTMENT

My favourite special occasion shoes are a pair I bought years ago. They are the Jimmy Choo Lance heel and I've worn them so much their cost per wear is almost free at this stage! I'd say I've worn them about thirty times to various events and weddings. They go with everything and the leather in them is soft as butter – and we all know how important comfort is in shoes when you're going to be in them for a full day or night. I knew I would wear them a lot, but I didn't think they'd be as comfortable as they are. They sit on your foot in a really flattering way and even though they're strappy the way the strap sits under your ankle means that they never cut into you and they really elongate the leg. They're the definition of a good investment.

I bought the matching bag too, and I basically use that every time I wear the shoes.

My investment earrings are from a brand called Soru that I really love and although they look like a big statement piece they work well with almost everything. The gold goes with all colours and I've worn them with evening dresses and with a t-shirt and jeans during the day. I think almost everything can be dressed down in a really cool way.

ACCESSORIES

It's an old trope that you can completely change an outfit with an accessory, and while I don't think it's completely true, I do think that scarves and bags are really important to finishing a look and possibly hiding the truth of an outfit. For example, you could be on your way to the school run looking absolutely shocking, but if you throw your nice winter coat over your jeans and old t-shirt, wrap a really nice scarf around your neck and put your favourite cross-body bag on, nobody is any the wiser. Or if you've been living in jeans, t-shirt and blazer for four days and haven't the energy to come up with a different outfit, a cool scarf and a change of bag will make you look like you've put in the effort.

Ever since having the boys I've only been buying cross-body bags. You always need to have a hand free with giddy boys around and you need enough room for at least one snack in there. Like everything else in my wardrobe, I think that if you have nice things you should use them so I change up my handbags all the time. I try to rotate them so that they all get an outing. Some days I could be wearing a designer bag with a bargain high-street outfit – but I think that's the fun of fashion, I love mixing it all up.

The same goes for scarves. I'm a big lover of them because I think they inject a bit of personality into an outfit and often add some much-needed colour. I think we could all do with some colour around our faces, particularly in the winter when we all tend to wear a lot of black or grey, and a scarf can be a quick way of doing that. I have a couple of beautiful ones that belonged to my mum and lots of inexpensive ones that I've picked up because I love the colour or the print.

OUT OUT

More often than not, unless it's a formal occasion, out out for me these days starts with a pair of Saturday Nights or Leather Look POCOs. These, teamed with a sparkly top and a pair of great heels, are really all I need. But I want to talk about our out out wardrobes. Most of us have a stockpile of sequin tops or beautiful dresses that only get worn a couple of times a year, and isn't that sad?

I think we all need to change the way we categorize our wardrobes so that we get more use out of our clothes. If you have a stunning sequin skirt that you love in December, you can still love it in February but with a grey cashmere jumper tucked in and a pair of trainers instead of killer heels. You can layer beautiful light summer dresses over tights and ankle boots and under a chunky knit, so that the print you loved in August can still be worn in October. We have to learn to wear what we have in a more creative way. I also need to remember that I live in Ireland and our seasons can be all over the place, so learning to layer should be a skill taught in school here!

CHAPTER NINE

Denim for Days

It'll come as no surprise to you when I say that jeans make up a huge part of my wardrobe. But even before I started POCO, denim was my one true fashion love.

I had known for a long time that I wanted to do my own thing when it came to clothes. I didn't want to do a full fashion collection, I wanted to focus on one thing, so I kept asking myself what do I love? What do I like wearing? Where do I see a niche in the market? And the answer was staring me in the face. I love denim.

The first thing I did was set about figuring out what didn't work. I'd always find a pair that I really liked, but which was wrong in some tiny way. The rise wasn't right, the fit of the leg was off, I didn't love the hardware on them. And I always felt that shopping for jeans had a bad reputation, it always seemed to come up as one of the retail experiences that everyone hated and I wanted to change that perception.

Back in the day I used to spend money on jeans, sometimes quite a lot of money, and I'd literally have to lie down on the bed and zip them up with a hanger. Up until a few years ago denim was very rigid and stiff. That was one of the first things I wanted to change. I wanted the fabric to feel nice, for everything to have a really good power stretch (that's the technical term!) but to still go back into shape. The emphasis with POCO is always on the quality and the fit.

HOW I WEAR DENIM

THE TUMMY TUCK

I could sing the praises of this style all day long. If you're not feeling your best these will help improve things. They're a higher rise that helps suck everything in and have a really flattering slim leg. I love these with a loose top half tucked in (the French Tuck we're all now so familiar with thanks to Tan on *Queer Eye*) and a block heel. I wear these all the time, both dressed up and down, and they're a great confidence booster.

THE JENNY

One of our newer styles, the Jenny, is what you'd call a mom jean. The phrase 'mom jean' can sound like quite an intimidating fashion term but what it really means is that they have a more relaxed fit and are a great midrise. These are brilliant at the weekend with trainers and a blazer, but I wanted to show them with a heel and a more professional look too so you can see how versatile they are. A sock boot with a slightly looser fit leg is really flattering as it shows a slim ankle.

THE CITY CROP

I am obsessed with this style. These have a straight leg so they're very flattering to wear. They skim over your knees and calves, so if they're the reason you hate skinny jeans these are the ones for you. They stop at the ankle, which we haven't been used to for a while but is a very flattering place for your jeans to stop. Your ankle is the slimmest point of your leg so you're drawing the eye to that instead of another point that you may not be thrilled about. These are great with a heel (low or high) and a t-shirt for a cool 'I sort of made an effort but I'm still really relaxed' look.

THE BOYF

These are basically the weekend in a jean. Soft, relaxed and effortless. If you reach for sportswear or leggings for comfort every Saturday, these are the perfect jeans for you. They're so easy to wear and look great with almost everything. The beauty of these is that they're comfortable without looking sloppy. They're a relaxed fit but still have a shape, which means you don't actually look like you've raided your boyfriend's wardrobe. These are good with a trainer or a heeled boot and are my favourites for hanging out with my boys.

THE OFF-DUTY JACKET

Double denim used to be such a fashion no-no and the only people who wore
it were dads trying to be cool. Thankfully that's all changed and I'm a big fan.
The key to wearing denim jackets is in the styling. This one has a relaxed fit
and looks great when you push the sleeves up to show your wrists and give
your silhouette some shape. I regularly team it with jeans but it looks great in
the summer over lightweight dresses and in winter under big heavy coats for
some stylish layering.

BUMP STYLE

I've had two babies. That's eighteen months of pregnancy and about ten months minimum of maternity clothes – and I found getting dressed in those ten months a nightmare.

When I was pregnant with Ollie I was only twenty-nine and I felt like an old woman. Everything was so dowdy and frumpy and not at all my style. I spent a little bit of money on Topshop or Asos maternity pieces but not much. I really didn't think there was a good enough selection out there. And if you had to go to an event it was a nightmare. Maternity things for occasions are so expensive and who wants to spend the money on something you'll just wear once?

Although I decided against doing a full maternity range with POCO, I did think I could help a little bit on that front and we created the Mama-to-Be and the Off-Duty Mama-to-Be jeans. I just kept thinking back to how I felt when I was pregnant – older than my years, frumpy. Any of the jeans I tried on then, even if they were a skinny fit, felt saggy. You feel bad enough as it is on a lot of days when you're pregnant, without your clothes adding to that negativity. That's why it was important to me to include maternity jeans in POCO. Ours are under the bump, they're neat but have amazing stretch and they're nice enough to wear after the baby comes when you're not ready to get back into your old jeans again. Most importantly you don't feel like a big frump in them!

CHAPTER TEN

Dressing Kids

I love dressing the boys, it's so much fun. I never thought I'd be the kind of mum that would dress her children the same, but sometimes I can't resist, it's just too cute.

It was only when we moved that I realized I'd been hanging on to way too much stuff for the kids and did a big clear-out (move house – it's the greatest purging exercise ever!). I've gotten rid of things that don't fit any more and anything that was damaged. I've kept a lot of Ollie's things that were still perfectly fine so Louis can wear them. I keep them in clear boxes with the age on them – there's my label maker again! – and they're ready to go. I did keep the really special things though – all of their 'firsts', like shoes and Babygros, but Ollie goes through shoes and runners at such a rate that everything after the first pair are just gone.

The boys grow so quickly that it's high street all the way for them. My favourites are M&S and Next, and now that Ollie's getting a bit bigger, I like Zara on him. They're such boys though, and they don't really like stiff jeans or buttons, they just get in the way of jumping around the place, so I'm always looking for things with elasticated waists for them. Even now that Ollie's six I still only tend to buy him softer fabrics with a stretchy waistband. I want them to be able to throw themselves around the place and not be worried about what they're wearing.

I'm all about an easy life when it comes to the boys so I love sweatshirts on them and cute t-shirts. I don't like dressing them older than their age, so I keep things simple. And I don't like putting black on babies, I prefer colour on kids, which is probably why I like ranges like Jools Oliver's *Little Bird* collection for Mothercare. It's really bright and sweet and it's very good quality.

Quality is important with clothes for children because they get washed so often. I think M&S have the best pyjamas for kids, they wash really well and while they are a little more expensive than in some other high street places they do last longer, which is better value in the long run.

Tips for dressing kids

* **Comfort is key.** *Soft fabrics are the best for soft, delicate skin.*

* **Don't spend too much money** *on clothes that will be grown out of quickly.*

* **Use colour.** *Kids can definitely get away with clashing colours and prints.*

* **Invest in shoes.** *The right footwear will ensure your child's feet grow correctly.*

FASHION INSTAGRAM ACCOUNTS I LOVE

Holly Willoughby @hollywilloughby

I love Holly's style and the outfit posts Holly puts up every day are pure inspo. She also seems like someone you'd totally want to go on a night out with! If you think Holly's wardrobe is goals you probably need to follow Angie Smith too (@angiesmithstyle), not only does she style Holly but she's worked with Rochelle Humes, Emma Bunton and our own Angela Scanlon and Laura Whitmore.

Louise Cooney @louisecooney_

Limerick girl Louise has the wardrobe of your dreams. But not only is she incredibly stylish, she's really nice too. Louise is a fashion star on the rise and this year had her own Nasty Gal edit. She's going global.

Anine Bing @aninebing

You don't get much cooler than this. Founder and chief creative officer of her own label, Anine's is the account to follow for examples of how to wear denim with style. Follow her for a peek into her very fashionable life, outfit inspo and the occasional glimpse of her very stylish kids.

Tezza @tezza

Following Tezza is basically like seeing a magazine editorial on Instagram every day. Her pictures are unbelievable, her style is incredible, and she even has her own editing app. Now that's finding your niche and going with it!

Emma Hill @emmahill

Londoner Emma has a signature style that she knows works for her. It's simple but cool and I love seeing how she puts understated looks together.

PART FOUR

Beauty

CHAPTER ELEVEN

My Beauty Secrets

People ask me if I've had cosmetic work done all the time.

It's one of the most regular questions I get asked and to be honest I take it as a compliment. The most common thing people ask me on Instagram is 'Where do you go for your lip fillers?' They don't even ask if I have lip fillers, they just assume I do! I mean, I am getting more wrinkled as I get older, like everyone, but I've always had pretty decent-looking lips. That's not to say that I wouldn't get them done in the future, but I don't think I need my lips filled – of all the things I could get done, they wouldn't be top of my list! I wouldn't be opposed to a bit of Baby Botox but I think we all need a 'less is more' approach.

I don't have a problem with the idea of cosmetic surgery, but what I don't like to see is really young girls getting work done when they don't need it. In general, I have a live and let live attitude to injectables – do what makes you happy. I just don't think Botox and fillers should be the first thing you go for. All it will do is paralyze the muscle or fill out a wrinkle and you could still have skin that looks terrible. If you're getting Botox over skin that you haven't looked after I actually think it can look worse.

Everyone should be focusing on a really good skincare routine before they consider going down the injectables route. If my best friend said to me 'Oh I got the works done', I'd say happy days, do what works for you – but I just don't think it should be the first line of defence. Every year there are so many amazing new treatments to try that don't involve putting anything into your skin, and experts say that things like microneedling and laser treatment can be just as effective as Botox when it comes to dealing with fine lines and ageing.

'Everyone should be focusing on a really good skincare routine before they consider going down the injectables route.'

SKINCARE

I've seen my skin change as I've been getting older so I'm putting in more of an effort to keep it looking well. Being around Jennifer Rock (The Skin Nerd) in the last few years has really helped me become educated about my skin and what we should all be doing, so I'm quite regimented in my skincare routine now. Here's what I do.

Before you even think about anything else the most basic thing to master is cleaning your face properly.

It sounds so simple but it will make a really big difference to how all the products you use afterwards are absorbed. Before I got into a routine of thoroughly cleaning my face, I didn't even realize that I wasn't doing it properly. There is a whole trend for the double cleanse and the pre-cleanse now – and it just means that you should clean your face twice. I think that if you're wearing make-up during the day you really want to cleanse twice every evening.

Think of the first cleanse as removing all your make-up and the second as actually cleaning your face. You don't need two products, just one cleanser – but do it twice. If you've ever had a facial you'll know how many times they clean your face and that's to make sure that all the steps that follow are 100 per cent effective, and you want to emulate that at home. Now, you might be thinking that you barely have time to run a wipe over your face, but honestly, it's the single thing you'll do that will make the most difference. Our skin regenerates at night, so a proper clean that preps your skin to soak in whatever you put on it while you sleep is the kindest thing you can do for your face. Well, that and SPF every day. If we taught everyone those two steps from when they're really young everyone's skin would be much better, for much longer.

I like using a balm or oil cleanser first as I find that really gets the muck off. It melts your make-up off so you're ready for the next step, and then what I use next depends on how my skin is that day. If it's feeling really dehydrated, I'll use a cream cleanser like the **Image Vital C Cleanser** as it's very hydrating. If I'm having a breakout, I'll use something that works specifically to treat and

calm my skin. If you can use a different product for your second cleanse, that one should be your treatment cleanser.

Once I've cleansed and cleaned my face, I'll use an eye cream and a serum. I often don't bother with a moisturizer over the top of the serum, which I know some people find surprising. If my skin could do with some comfort I might use a thick night cream, but most of the time I don't think it's essential. I prefer to spend my money on serums, because now I know that they are the ones doing all the work – they're what gets deep down through the layers of my skin and helps to regenerate cells.

In the morning, I have a cleanser in the shower that I use, but just once, and follow that with a serum and an SPF moisturizer. I use SPF every day, it really is essential. Environmental factors and sun damage cause the most harm to our skin, so we need to protect our faces from them as best we can. You can get really good sun protection for your face these days that contains a high factor but is thin enough to go under your make-up and not leave a chalky hue. Image Skincare do a great one but I also like ones from Chanel, Clarins and La Roche-Posay.

That's the skincare routine that I have found is effective for me. You have to get to know your skin, and if you can go to see a professional skincare expert you should. They'll tell you what type of skin you have and what you should use that will best suit it. There are great products available in chemists and on beauty counters, but you should really think about what type of skin you have first – it's easy to buy the wrong thing or self-diagnose incorrectly. Dehydrated skin is different from dry skin, and skin changes a lot as we age too. What may have been oily at one point can become dehydrated, or what was combination can become sensitive.

MICRONEEDLING

My current favourite skin treatment, microneedling, works by stimulating the production of new collagen in the skin. Microscopic needles work to puncture the skin and as the skin starts to heal itself it triggers the collagen production.

'I like to try new treatments every so often to supplement my skincare and I recently tried microneedling. I thought it was amazing! It made such a big difference. It was brilliant for skin texture and my lines were definitely softened.'

It treats blocked pores, minor scarring, sun damage and fine wrinkles, and it helps products applied after treatment to penetrate deeper into the skin.

THE SCIENCE

There are a lot of words and facts thrown about when it comes to beauty and skincare. Here's the lowdown on some of them.

VITAMIN C

Probably best known for fighting colds, vitamin C should also be part of your skincare routine. It provides very powerful antioxidant protection and is known for its anti-ageing benefits and for its skin-correcting properties. The sun, pollution and even the oxygen we breathe can cause damage to the skin and can result in inflammation, premature ageing and dehydration, which nobody wants. Vitamin C can help to:

* *reduce irritation and sensitivity*
* *stimulate collagen production*
* *reduce the appearance of scars and acne marks*
* *reduce the appearance of pigmentation and discolouration*

HYALURONIC ACID

Just a few years ago the idea of putting acid anywhere near our faces
would have sent us running for the hills but now we can't get enough of it.
Hyaluronic acid is the secret to hydrated skin. Our skin cells actually produce
this magical acid naturally, but ageing and environmental triggers mean that
those natural levels can take a dip which can cause fine lines, uneven texture
and dullness. A hyaluronic serum might become your best friend.

GLYCOLIC ACID

This is another of the hero acids. Its speciality is being able to penetrate layers
of skin to reveal the better skin underneath. It's also a teaching acid and can
train your skin to become better at retaining its natural moisture. It's part of
the AHA family (Alpha Hydroxy Acids) and when used on its own or with other
AHAs it can help to improve the skin's firmness. I like this acid in a cleanser.

VITAMIN A

This is a hero skin vitamin and you can apply it topically and get it through
your food. When it's applied in a cream form it's usually better known as
retinol and it stimulates the production of new cells. Most experts will tell
you that this is the skin vitamin that everyone needs. Foods high in vitamin A
include salmon, dairy products, eggs and cod liver oil.

CHAPTER TWELVE

Maintenance

Everyone's idea of the things they do as their basic maintenance is going to be different. I'm on stage a lot and can often be asked to do events last minute so I like to keep on top of my nails, hair and tan so I don't have to worry about it. I make it a priority and it's an essential part of my routine. But it's basically my job so you may not need as much maintenance as I do!

I find that it also helps when I'm having an off-duty day and don't want to bother with make-up and the works. If I have my basics in hand I still feel presentable.

I think as women we can be looked down on for going for a manicure or be hard on ourselves for making the time to get our hair done, but we should be making the time to look after ourselves. If it's not your nails you should do something else – meet a friend for coffee or do a yoga class. If it makes you feel good you should factor it in. If your partner can manage to play golf or go to a match or even get to the barber, you can get your nails done. Guilt free.

Here are my maintenance musts.

NAILS

I always have my nails done. I don't feel dressed without them and nine times out of ten I'm wearing Shellac or Gelish because they just don't budge. I really like nude or light pink nails and it can be hard to keep them from getting stained, but I was given a good tip: when you get your long-wear polish done in a pale colour, put a bit of clear polish over the top yourself and then every couple of days take that off and reapply it. You'd be surprised (and a little horrified) at the amount of dirt that comes off from tan, make-up and everything else.

BROWS

Do not, I repeat do not, underestimate the importance of having good brows. They really do completely change the shape of your face, and it's not like ten years ago when if you went to get your brows done they just did the same shape on everyone. Brow artists are amazing now. I have PhiBrows and it made such a difference. Kim O'Sullivan in the Dublin Make-up Academy did mine and she's brilliant. My brows are like a face foundation for me and I think they're such a time-saver too. People used to say 'Oh I wouldn't go anywhere without mascara' and now (well for me anyway) it's much more a case of I wouldn't go anywhere without my brows done.

TAN

I love my tan, it really helps me feel put together even on my very relaxed days. I never get a spray tan, I always do it myself, I'm a bit of a pro now. I even get Brian to do my back sometimes. I say 'Go on, put your big man-hand in the mitt there', he huffs and puffs and then he does it! Get a man that will tan your back and you know you've found true love!

I have a couple of tan brands that I love and use all the time. **Bondi Sands** and **Vita Liberata** would be two of my favourites but there are so many good tanning brands on the market now, it's brilliant.

I always have a face tan on too. I never use the same tan on my face as my body even if it says you can. I find the body ones drying and think they can cause breakouts. I adore a brand called **Tan Luxe** and they do special face drops. You add two or three drops to your moisturizer or serum at night-time

and you wake up with a really lovely glow. I bring that down onto my neck and then tan from the top of my chest down.

If you're not into the commitment of a full tan I think there are some great gradual tanners that you can try. During the summer, a bit of the **Dove Summer Revived** gradual tanner on your legs every second day instead of your usual moisturizer will give you a little colour and some glow without the effort of fake tan.

My other tan secret is for when I have my legs out. I tan them as normal and then, if I have an event or I'm going somewhere, I use **Vita Liberata Body Blur** – it's Photoshop in a bottle and I love it. I stipple it on with a foundation brush and it works miracles. If you've ever seen me out at an event or on stage at a Fashion Factory, that's what I have on my legs. Then, if I'm going all out, like going on *The Late Late Show*, I'll also have **Charlotte Tilbury Supermodel Body** down the centre of my shins. It's a gorgeous product that gives this amazing glow and I really think it lengthens your legs. It's a great combination that everyone should know about and it's perfect for big events like a wedding or for Christmas parties when you really want to look fabulous.

HAIR

One of the best things I've done with my hair in recent years is getting **Rapture** extensions. Tracey at Peter Mark does them for me and one of the reasons I love them is because they're so quick to apply. They're on tape so it's a much faster experience than bonds, which can take hours to get in. They can be applied in fifteen minutes and out again in five. I don't get them for length, I have them for volume and I love the look of them.

These days I'm styling my hair much less than I used to because I just don't think it's good for my hair, especially when I'm dying it all the time. I get it coloured every eight weeks or so and that can be a lot for hair to take so I'm cutting back with heat styling to try and give it a break.

I've also had a problem with the water in the house, it was turning my hair green, which was a disaster – so I hadn't been washing it a huge amount at home. (I've since gotten a filter, which seems to have done the trick.) Dry shampoo is my best friend. I also really like textured hair so I've been testing all the brands trying to find the best one.

The best dry shampoos

1. *Oribe – expensive but amazing. Maybe not for every day.*

2. *Ouai by Jen Atkin. This is the line by Chrissy Teigen's stylist and I really like it. It's very light and really works.*

3. *Kevin Murphy Bedroom Hair is lovely and the smell is unreal!*

4. *Morrocanoil has a dry shampoo specifically for blondes called Light Tones that works brilliantly to lighten up the root area. I also really love Colour Wow to help on days that you have terrible roots or a lot of grey – I've had greys for over twenty years so something like this is an essential. I use the Platinum Blonde one. They also have a product called Dream Coat that gives a really smooth finish and makes home blow-drying a pleasure.*

STYLING

When I do style my hair, I love a wave. It's such a good tip for second- and third-day hair that needs to be refreshed. A little dry shampoo, a texturizing product and a wave is the best way of injecting life into your hair.

I think the trick to getting the perfect wave and not having it look too set or too 'done' is to keep the ends straight. You leave them out altogether when you're using your tool and that's the way to get the perfect beachy, undone look. Joanne Kelly is an amazing stylist and she's the queen of the wave. If you ever watch her on Instagram doing waves she will always advise leaving the ends out – it's the best way to make it look like you didn't make an effort – when we know you really did.

My favourite tool is the **Hot Tools Curl Bar**, I love the shape of it. It's very easy to use yourself because it's just the one barrel. I just wrap the centre section around it and move it up and down a little. Nothing at the root and nothing at the end. You want to work so that the waves go away from your face, which helps to open it up. Once you get away from your face you can do some pieces in the opposite direction to break it up a little and then you swap hands for the other side. It really is simple. It's not an expensive tool either, about €60, and it really works.

If you're someone who does a lot of blow-drying at home it is worth investing in a good-quality hairdryer. I have a Dyson, and even though it's expensive it really is worth it. It's very light, gives you a very smooth finish and doesn't overheat, which is great for your hair – you won't get static or frizzy hair and it's very fast. Anything that manages to do all that, and avoids a trip to the salon, is worth it in my book. Another great and affordable option is the LanaiBLO hairdryer – it's a salon-quality hairdryer.

CHAPTER THIRTEEN

Make-up

I have two very different make-up routines. One for work and stage, and one for everyday life. I love make-up, I love discovering new products and I love playing about at my dressing table. Maybe it's because I live in a house full of boys, but my make-up table is a refuge for me, my girly space.

EVERYDAY

My everyday routine is quick and simple. Because I wear so many heavy products when I'm at work I like to keep it light, and recently I've gotten into BB or CC creams instead of a foundation. They're lightweight, some of them are corrective, and they take about two minutes to put on.

At the moment, I really like the **IT Cosmetics CC Cream** and the **Jane Iredale Glow Time**. After my base I always put on some under-eye concealer and some nude eyeliner. I have two children so anything that helps my eyes look rested and less tired is an essential item for me. Your waterline (lower lash line) is naturally red so a nude liner will make your eyes look bigger, brighter and more awake.

I love a good mascara. Everyone is looking for something different from a mascara so find the one that suits you. If I am putting anything on my eyes, I'll do a sweep of bronzer over my cheeks and then put a little of that over my lids as a shadow. It's an easy way of making your look cohesive without too much effort.

A QUICK CHANGE

If I'm going to an event straight from work and need to update my make-up I usually concentrate on my eyes. You can touch up your foundation pretty easily but if you're not taking it all off and putting it all back on again the easiest way to look done without too much effort is by doing an eye.

Stila have a product called **Magnificent Metals** that are great for this. They go on as a liquid but dry really quickly and even just a sweep of that across your lids will make you look like you've had your eyes done professionally. If it's an evening event and I want a bit more drama I'll use eyeliner too.

I'm not great with liquids or doing flicked lines so I tend to go for really nice soft kohl pencils that I apply right down at the root of the lashes and smudge out for a soft smoky effect.

'I think concealer should be a shade or two lighter than your foundation to help brighten the area. But be careful not to go too bright, you don't want the reverse panda look.'

BIN IT

I'm very passionate about doing make-up clear-outs. Don't hold on to mascaras for more than three months trying to get every last bit out of them. They just dry up and clump up and they're not good for your eyes. I'd always buy a more affordable mascara that you don't feel bad about throwing out and changing it up all the time. I found out about the little 6m or 12m stamps on the bottom of products a few years ago. Before that I never realized that make-up went off. It will tell you on the bottom how many months the product will last for once you open it. When the air gets to a product it can start to oxidize and go off. You're also putting a brush or your finger into them day-in day-out which, when you think about it, isn't very sanitary.

Once I found out I started to mention it at the Fashion Factories and people were shocked. We often have a habit of saving things for 'special use' and using just a little bit every so often to make it last but it's actually not worth doing. You can often tell that products have gone off. Foundations will start to get discoloured or separate, moisturizers can get harder, even your perfume will go off if you leave it in the light.

I'm lucky that brands often send me things to test but I'm getting better at clearing things out now. I give things to my sister and the girls in the office to test instead of using things once and holding on to them. It's such a waste in the long run.

My holy grail products

*   *Charlotte Tilbury's Nude Eyeliner:* to fake a good night's rest.

*   *Foundations by NARS:* they've just nailed the foundation game, they're all stunning.

*   *Liquid Lipsticks by Charlotte Tilbury:* another vote for Charlotte. A lot of liquid lipsticks can be drying and flaky but hers are lovely.

*   *First Aid Beauty Coconut Skin Smoothie:* I use this a lot, it's great under foundation but I also wear it on its own if I have a little tan on my face. It has a lovely glow.

*   *Complete Concealer by NARS:* this is great if you have some blemishes you need to clear up.

*   *Urban Decay Naked Skin:* this is such a good under-eye concealer, definitely worth the hype.

*   *Studio Fix Concealer by MAC:* this is a great under-eye concealer for days when you need extra help. It's heavy and covers a lot but manages not to cake.

*   *Laura Mercier Loose Setting Powder:* it has a cult status for a reason, it really is just the best.

*   *Soleil Tan de Chanel:* this is such a lovely product and I've been using it for years. You can put it under or over your foundation for a really natural sun-kissed glow. Gorgeous.

FRAGRANCE

Scents are so personal aren't they? They can bring up so many memories. My mum always wore **Chanel N°5** and sometimes if I get a whiff of that from someone else it can instantly make me upset. She was always dripping in **Elnett** and N°5, and even now when I'm doing my hair and spray Elnett it can knock me sideways for a minute.

At the moment, I'm wearing a lot of **Matière Noire by Louis Vuitton**, it's a really luxurious scent and I love it. When I first met Brian I wore **Coco Mademoiselle** a lot and that's what I wore on our wedding day. Now when I wear it he always says 'hello Coco'. It's kind of our scent.

'Scents can really bring you back to a special place, time or person.'

MY GLAM SQUAD

It takes a village to help me look the way I do for big events, and a huge part of that village are my very favourite hair and make-up artists.

It's so important when you're working with people that, apart from them being really good at their jobs, everyone is on the same wavelength. I try to avoid working with people who panic or get really fussy. I'm quite relaxed and easy-going, so I don't want anyone who makes a big deal out of things because it would make me stressed. Our team is small and we work really closely with each other, so everyone has to be on the same vibe and the glam squad are a huge part of that. I work with them at Fashion Factories, they help me get ready for events and, apart from anything else, they're my friends.

Aimee Connolly: Make-up

Aimee is such a gifted make-up artist – and she's quick which, if you get your face painted as often as I do, is great! She really reminds me of myself. She's always doing 20 million things at once! We had her in the POCO pop-up shop in Liffey Valley last year with her **Sculpted** palette and I was delighted to have her there. It was the first time we had another brand in the store and it worked really well. Sometimes I forget how young Aimee is, she's only twenty-six, as she has such a great business mind. I can't wait to see where she is in five or ten years.

David Cashman: Hair

I've known David since I was twelve. We went to school together and he was actually the first person to colour my hair. That time, it was orange, and whatever we were using we shouldn't have been – it was probably **Sun-in** – so he's definitely come a long way! David comes to Fashion Factories and also helps me get ready for shoots and events. I love having him around, he's so talented, but he's also hilarious and a great dancer!

Joanne Kelly: Hair

The queen of the wave! Joanne is a brilliant hair stylist who can make you feel so fabulous. She's so in demand, but if I can have her on a shoot with me, I will. Apart from being incredibly skilled she also has the most beautiful Instagram where she shows lots of inspo and you get a glimpse of her gorgeous little boys. She's also building a house and her interior posts are next level.

Sarah Keary: Make-up

Sarah is another make-up artist who I love. She did my face for the Blossom Tree Ball and I thought it was gorgeous. She has a really light touch and can make you look like the most beautiful version of yourself. Such a talent.

Tara Anderson: Make-up

I love Tara – she does loads of the make-up demos at the Fashion Factories and it's great being on stage with her because she's a scream. It's so important when you're up there in front of people that you have banter, and she's just so funny. If you don't know Tara, you would think she's such a lady. She's so beautiful and preened, but then she starts to talk and you never know what she'll come out with – I love that. She also has the most infectious laugh. And as well as all that, she's also a brilliant make-up artist.

LET'S HEAR IT FROM THE GLAM SQUAD

Aimee Connolly @aimeeconnolly_com

I've had the pleasure of working with Pippa over the last few years between her Fashion Factories, events and general outings and it's always so much fun. Apart from her gorgeous face, she is so lovely to be around, doesn't take herself too seriously and it's great to be able to say that we're actually friends now.

Pippa and I share the same love of simple, effortless-looking make-up (which actually involves a lot of product and time). I would say our signature style is a dewy, glowing skin and a soft smoky eye to complement it. A style that makes you look enhanced but everyone knows is still you.

My desert island make-up bag

I couldn't live without a nice, glowing base for the skin, a good under-eye concealer, a brow mascara gel, my **Sculpted** palette with cream highlighter and lip liner. Lip liner for me is an absolute must and something I would almost favour over a lipstick.

My pro tip

It might sound basic, but my biggest philosophy when it comes to make-up and all things beauty is that less is more. Lighten up on the amount of products you're using, how much of those products you're applying, and also how heavy handed you're being. These all make a difference in terms of creating a gorgeous, natural make-up style that still looks like you.

How I make up on the move

I do a lot of travelling or just general running around and so I need things that are quick and handy, which is totally reflected in my range. I use my **Beauty**

Base every day, which I launched at the start of this year. It's a moisturizing primer with SPF 30+ and hyaluronic acid, and leaves your skin with a golden glow. This and cream highlighter on top of your make-up are a godsend for fresh, radiant skin. I always use my finger to tap my cream highlighter onto the tip of the cheekbones, down the centre of the nose and along the Cupid's bow – you will look instantly more revived and it's perfect on all ages too.

David Cashman @cashmandjmc

A day working with Pippa honestly never feels like work and is always an enjoyable time. You're guaranteed a laugh . . . or six. Not only does Pippa keep it exciting with her variety of jobs from POCO campaigns, to magazine cover shoots, to chatting all things hair at her Fashion Factories, but she always keeps it fun and it's never dull – that's for sure!

What I do to Pippa's hair

I spray **L'Oreal Tecni Art Pli** onto damp hair at the roots and blow dry. Then I take a **Babyliss Pro Curler** and slide it down through big sections, leaving the ends out so it's not too curly. Then I shake it all out and finish it with a light texture spray.

My desert island hair tool

If I'm on a desert island I'm not bringing any hair tools – I'd be going full on Tom Hanks in **Cast Away**!

Actually no, salty water and my hair? Can I grab a moisture mask and a comb? And sure, Tom Hanks too, while you're at it!

My pro tip

Invest in a decent hairdryer. Also, like make-up brushes our hairbrushes need to be kept clean too. It's pointless drying clean hair with a dirty brush, so take out the old hair gathered in it and give it a soak in soapy water once a week.

My Pippa Secret (I've known her since school)

She's not a natural blonde, lol!

Joanne Kelly @joannekellyhair

One of the main reasons I love working with Pippa is the fact that she trusts professionals and values their opinions, which makes the process easy, creative and completely stress-free. She is also a very relaxed, chilled-out person so working with her is usually a lovely day out! It also helps that she's gorgeous, so no matter what we do with her we can't really go wrong!

What I use in Pippa's hair

I use **L'Oreal Tecni Art Pli** for every style. Spray at the start and blow-dry into hair for hold. Then I use a **T3 Clip Barrel** (I use the small size on Pippa, the medium on mine because my hair is a little longer) and lots of texture sprays. My favourites are **Unite – Texturiza**, **Moroccanoil Dry Texture Spray** and **Joico Body Shake**!

My desert island hair tool

My absolute favourite hair tool is my **T3 Interchangeable Barrel**. There is an attachment for every hair type and you can create everything from soft curls to beachy waves.

My pro tip

The biggest tip I can give people is that in order to make their waves last longer, you need to leave them alone for at least twenty minutes after curling. The more time they have to cool down, the longer they will last. After that you can brush them out to soften them. Another tip to create Pippa's effortless, relaxed waves is to leave the ends straight. This gives the hair a more casual feel.

Tara Anderson @tara_makeup

We started off modelling together back in the day and hit it off immediately. We both have a similar sense of humour so working together never feels like work as we usually get very giddy, especially on stage at the Fashion Factories.

How I do Pippa's face

As we all know, Pippa is naturally very beautiful, so doing her make-up is very easy. I usually go for very glowy skin and a soft smoky eye. Pippa is extremely easy-going, which is always great as a make-up artist – she trusts you to do your thing.

My desert island make-up bag

It's so hard to narrow down my absolute must-have make-up products. **Charlotte Tilbury Eye Cheat** is definitely a make-up bag essential, it gives the illusion of a full night's sleep and is the quickest way to make your eyes look bigger and brighter. **Rimmel Wonder'Full Brow** gel is a brilliant quick fix for thickening up sparse brows and adding some natural definition. Everybody asks for airbrushed-looking skin these days and I find **Benefit's Porefessional** amazing for achieving a flawless, poreless finish to the skin.

Powder or cream highlighter?

I would say my preference for highlighter will always be powder, I just prefer the finish and think it's much easier for make-up novices too. A gorgeous way to add glow to your skin is to mix a liquid illuminator in with your foundation. A favourite of mine is **Charlotte Tilbury Hollywood Flawless Filter**, it gives the most beautiful subtle glow.

My pro tip

You can buy the most expensive foundation on the market but if your skin isn't prepped you won't get the best result. For a quick boost of hydration, I love massaging **Trilogy Rosehip Oil** on the skin before foundation. It is like giving your skin a big drink of water and I guarantee you will get a better finish from your foundation.

How I fake sleep!

As a new mum I have never had such little sleep. It is amazing how much you can function on a couple of hours. I have had to go for a full coverage for my under-eye concealer these past few months. I find **Urban Decay All Nighter** gives an extremely good coverage and **Bourjois Healthy Mix Concealer** is a great affordable one too.

Sarah Keary @sarahkearymakeup

Pippa is a make-up artist's dream. Her skin is the perfect canvas to work on. She lets me do what I want to explore my creativity. We always have lots of fun on set too!

How I do Pippa's face

Pippa always asks me for my signature 'fresh glowy' look. I start with a medium-coverage flawless base, introduce a little contour and light, rosy blush and finish off with a dewy highlighter. I then create softly blended smoky eyes, defined with liner and individual lashes. We then perfect her pout with a natural lip, nude lipstick and lashings of gloss.

My desert island make-up bag

This is a difficult question as I am surrounded by so many products. However, I could never live without **Kiehl's Ultra Facial Moisturizer** for hydration, **MAC Studio Fix Powder**, a slick coat of **Benefit BADGal Bang! Mascara** and **Hourglass Lip Treatment Oil** with rose pigment.

How I do my signature subtle, glowy look

It's all about the tools of the trade. I am obsessed with using the best brushes that ensure a flawless finish. My approach is to accentuate people's best features and let their natural beauty shine through. I am great believer in simplicity and less is more.

My pro tip

I have many tips but one that immediately springs to mind is when you're in a rush, winged eyeliner is always the first thing that can go wrong. Correct any smudges or mistakes by dipping a (recyclable) cotton bud in eye make-up remover and use this to sharpen your wing. And I can't stress enough how important it is to hydrate from the inside out, so remember to drink plenty of water!

PART FIVE

Travel

CHAPTER FOURTEEN

Getting Away

I love to travel, it's always been a big part of my life. I go away a lot for work but I also love getting away with Brian, with my friends, and these days I especially love to travel with the boys. Well, I love it when I'm there, I'm not sure anyone really loves travelling with small children.

I think because I'm away so much I have a very relaxed attitude to the airport. Others might use different words for my attitude, but let's call it relaxed. I usually get to the gate just before the plane takes off, and I've had a couple of near misses! But, really, that's just when I only have to worry about myself. When we're going as a family I'm much more responsible, I swear.

HOW I PACK

When it's just me I usually pack for myself at the last minute. Because I'm always working and that involves being on show, when we go on holidays I'm quite basic and keep things very low key. Especially when I have the boys with me. I'll bring make-up but I'll rarely put it on and I won't really wear heels, so my personal packing for a break in the sun is really pretty easy. I use my rail and hang up the pieces I think I want to bring and edit it from there. I try to remember that I don't need as much as I think, especially when it's a family holiday. I want to be as relaxed as possible with the boys so I simplify my rail before I fill my case. It's a different story if it's a trip with friends or a weekend in London with Brian. In that case, I pull outfits for nights out and accessorize those first – I find seeing complete outfits together a huge help – and then I choose some daytime looks with comfort in mind. I'll always leave a little room in the bag for coming home, just in case I happen to pick something up.

If we're all going I usually pack for the boys a week or two beforehand. I usually take out everything I'm thinking of bringing for them out and put it on the spare bed, then I spend a few days going in and looking at them. I don't pack twenty t-shirts and twenty pairs of shorts, I pack things as an outfit so I lay things out that way. I have found in the past that I've packed far too much for them so I'm really careful now.

If we're going on a sun holiday where they'll be in the pool most of the day I know that they won't need much. They each have a hooded towel that goes over their head like a poncho and they'll wear that to have their lunch and everything. They don't really tend to get changed so I actually need much less than I initially think. Mainly it's swimming gear and an outfit each for the evening. I love them in matching clothes on holidays – it's so hard to resist – so when I find outfits in both their sizes I get them. They're young; I'm sure when they're bigger they'll let me know that matchy-matchy time is over! I've actually matched the boys and Brian on occasion too, though I don't think I'll get away with that again!

WHAT I PACK

Now that I've cleared out my ten-year-old holiday drawer I'm trying to be more discerning about what I buy. Of course, I still pick up bits from the high street but now I look out for more classic things that I know I'll be able to keep for a long time. I'm also adding some better quality pieces that are staples. I don't want to be back in a situation where lots of cheaper things are going to recycling or charity after each summer. We all need to think a bit more carefully about waste, and getting rid of stuff each year isn't the way to go.

What I've invested in are some nice hats (it's easy to pack them without squishing them completely – just roll up underwear and bikinis and put them in the hat to keep the shape and then pack around it), a good swimsuit, a pair of soft leather sandals because there's nothing worse than a pair of cheap sandals cutting the feet off you for a week, and a couple of nice kaftans, especially if you spend the majority of your holiday around the pool.

For swimwear, I love brands like Seafolly and this year I got a lovely Calvin Klein one that I'll have for years.

'I wear swimsuits on holidays and people often ask me why I don't wear bikinis: the honest answer is that I'm not that confident wearing one. Maybe because I breastfed the two boys I don't feel like I have good enough boobs to wear a bikini. I feel like I get more of a lift in a swimsuit, it gives you a better shape. I feel too flat in a bikini, like my stomach is the same as my top half. I would have worn them more before I had kids, definitely, and I wish I didn't care as much, but I feel better in a one-piece and you know what, that's fine. They're also really fashionable at the moment so that helps.'

TRAVELLING WITH KIDS

We've become pretty good at getting Ollie and Louis from Dublin Airport to our destination smoothly and a lot of it comes down to attitude. I've done a lot of travelling with them, including flying to LA with Ollie on my own!

We took Ollie away when he was a few weeks old and we did the same with Louis. I think the earlier you go away with kids, the more confident you'll be doing it in the future. If you're worried about it, just bite the bullet and do it early if you can. Book somewhere with a short enough flight and even if it goes wrong it'll be over in no time. We've had bad flights with both of them at different times and you just don't know when it will hit. Some of the longer flights we've done, or trips when I was on my own, which I thought would be disasters turned out just fine. Then sometimes when we've all been together they've had complete meltdowns. It's very hard. You sweat and you think everyone's looking at you, but you just have to not care too much when you're travelling with children and if someone's giving you the stink eye – shame on them. Most people are kind and understanding and you definitely get the sympathy eyes from other mums which helps.

You just have to try not to care because if you care too much you'll never go anywhere. Obviously, you don't want to cause difficulties for other people, but a crying baby is just a fact of life and most people can deal with it just fine.

My aeroplane kit

1. Buy some new toys. I pick up little things the boys haven't seen before in Tiger or the Euro Shop to keep them entertained. I introduce one new toy about once every hour on a long-haul flight and maybe a little less on a shorter one.

2. Snacks, snacks and more snacks. I bring raisins, baby biscuits, bananas and yoghurt pouches. Lollipops are great too because they last for ages. You seriously can't bring enough treats.

3. If your child is older, like Ollie, I find downloading some of their favourite cartoons onto a tablet is a great way of keeping them occupied. Just make sure it's fully charged, your fastest way to a meltdown is promising Peppa and not being able to deliver!

4. Let your child pack their own on-board bag – it involves them and gets them excited. I also explain what the day will be like and what we'll be doing each step of the way, I find it helps manage expectations. I also explain the seat belt and the importance of safety in the hopes it will keep them in their seats at the right times.

5. Bring a favourite blanket or comforter for snuggles. Long-haul or early-morning/evening flights especially call for cosy naps.

6. A good bag. This is for you, not for them. You really want to make the flight and airport security go as smoothly as you can. A good nappy bag with compartments will really help. Even if your children are older, dig yours out and use it for the journey.

7. Finally, if you have a smallie bring more vests and nappies than you think you'll need. I'm not sure what it is about the plane but you're pretty much guaranteed a poonami. We had one with Louis where I just had to bin his vest and thankfully I had a few backups in the bag. There is seriously nothing worse.

CHAPTER FIFTEEN

The Ultimate Travel Guide

I definitely have some favourites when it comes to travel. Family holidays in Portugal have become our thing now. There's a really easy direct flight from Dublin to Faro, which is about ninety minutes from where we usually stay, and it works really well for children. Our usual holiday spot is incredibly well set up for families and you can get everything you need there from formula to sterilizers and everything in between. I love it when Brian, Ollie, Louis, Chloe my stepdaughter, and I get to all go together. It's such a relaxed place and it's lovely to be able to go somewhere that caters so well for us all and that we all love. It's hard to find a destination that's as good for a six-year-old as it is for an eighteen-year-old (and a 35-year-old!).

When it comes to romance you can't beat Paris. Brian and I have been a couple of times, we even did a babymoon there, and it never disappoints. But if I had to pick one place that covers a family break, a romantic getaway or a trip with the girls, I'd have to pick Dubai. I know some people hate it and think it's too man-made but I love it because you're guaranteed everything. You get the weather, there are hotels that cater for everything from over-the-top luxury to perfect family breaks. You can have adventure, shopping, great food and the beach. And apart from anything else I feel really safe there, so I love going as a family.

If you're planning a getaway, here are some of my favourite spots.

'Travel is an investment in yourself.'

DUBLIN

Even if you're from Dublin sometimes a weekend with the girls in your own hometown can be the best thing. Book into a hotel, go for brunch, do a little shopping, book an amazing dinner, organize a table for drinks and walk back to your room for a post-mortem and laughs. Twenty-four or forty-eight hours with your besties is sometimes all the medicine you need. If you're not from Dublin you can throw in a little sightseeing and you'll have the perfect weekend.

I'd start with brunch. Sometimes it seems like everyone on Instagram in Dublin is a professional bruncher and the city does have some amazing places to choose from. If the boys are at home I'll be getting myself a mimosa and having something delicious before I get on with the day.

Depending on who's with me I might go shopping – and for me that starts with Brown Thomas. There's such a variety of brands there, but I'll definitely have a little look at RIXO and the shoe department before popping upstairs to visit the Pippa Collection candles in homewares. I also love the Maria Tash piercing rooms. I've had a couple done now and I'm always on the lookout for more lovely pieces. If I'm on the other side of the city I'll head to Arnotts. Their beauty hall is unreal at the moment and they stock so many of the brands that Jennifer Rock (The Skin Nerd) recommends so I'll definitely have a browse there.

Dublin is a great city to walk around because it's so compact, so if I'm with someone who doesn't know it too well I'll have a stroll around, especially if the sun is shining. It's so nice walking up Grafton Street and getting a coffee to take to St Stephen's Green if the weather is good. If we fancy doing something touristy I might go to the Guinness Storehouse for the gorgeous views from the Gravity Bar and some pint-pulling fun. If the boys are with me the Natural History Museum is a must – it's fascinating in there.

On a girls' weekend it'll be back to the hotel to get ready before we head out for dinner. There are so many good places to eat but for a fun night out,

WILDE in the Westbury or The Ivy are great options and both are really central. If I'm out out in Dublin I'm definitely going to either House or 37 Dawson Street for cocktails and maybe even a bit of dancing.

STAY

* *The Shelbourne has been an iconic landmark in Dublin for nearly 200 years. Overlooking St Stephen's Green in the heart of the city, this five-star hotel is a must-visit if you're coming to Dublin. It has an amazing spa too.*

* *The Dylan is a five-star boutique hotel and is also within walking distance of the city centre. Based in Ballsbridge, it's also really close to the RDS Arena so an ideal stay if you're going to an event/concert there. We've had our Christmas party there in the past and it was a great choice.*

* *Located on Harcourt Street, The Dean is the best place to stay if you fancy enjoying what Dublin's nightlife has to offer. The interiors are really chic and modern and the rooms are really nice.*

* *The Marker has to be one of Dublin's most luxurious five-star hotels. With a modern design and rooms boasting gorgeous views of the Grand Canal, this Docklands hotel is one of my favourites. If the weather's nice, make sure to enjoy a drink on the rooftop terrace.*

* *Situated just off Grafton Street, The Westbury is another iconic hotel in the city. It has spacious rooms as well as restaurants and a spa, and it's worth grabbing a seat in the lounge, having a cup of tea and soaking up the luxurious surroundings. There's always a really warm and welcoming atmosphere at The Westbury.*

EAT

* *Having opened in 2018, **The Ivy** has quickly become the must-visit place in Dublin. Whether you come here for breakfast, lunch or dinner, the food is to die for. My favourite dish on the menu has to be the prawn curry. The interiors are absolutely stunning and the ladies' bathrooms are seriously Instagram-worthy.*

* ***Balfes** is an absolute gem. It's located inside The Westbury Hotel and is an all-day bistro. Again, it's perfect for breakfast, lunch or dinner (you need to try the BodyByrne pancakes). Its outdoor terrace is the ideal spot to sit and people-watch.*

* *Also in The Westbury Hotel is **WILDE**, which is the perfect restaurant to go to for date night. With gorgeous food and equally gorgeous interiors, it's definitely worth booking a table by the window.*

* *If you're into tapas and sharing plates, **Fade Street Social** is a great place to come with your friends. There's always a really vibrant atmosphere and a delicious cocktail menu.*

* *Mexican food lovers need to pay a visit to **777**. This Mexican restaurant and tequila cocktail bar could be easily missed on George Street with its low-key black exterior, but its funky and fun vibe inside, as well as the yummy food, make it totally worth seeking out.*

PARTY

* ***House Dublin** occupies two Georgian town houses on Leeson Street, close to St Stephen's Green. This is one of my favourite places to come for drinks with my friends. It has quite a relaxed*

vibe during the day/early evenings, and is always buzzing with people as the night goes on.

* *9 Below is a hidden gem just off St Stephen's Green. It has a moody, luxurious atmosphere with the best cocktails!*

* *Set over two floors, with four bars throughout, 37 Dawson Street is always a great place to go for a night out. The cocktails never disappoint, and the music is always on point. You're guaranteed a great night out!*

* *Sophie's is a rooftop restaurant/bar on the top floor of The Dean Hotel, offering 360-degree views of Dublin. Sunset views here have to be my absolute favourite.*

* *The Sidecar Bar in The Westbury Hotel is an award-winning cocktail bar that's the perfect spot for a pre-dinner drink. With its 1930s-inspired interiors, it's one of my favourite spots in the city.*

SHOP

* *Grafton Street is lined with almost every high-street store you can think of. From River Island to Marks & Spencer and Topshop, you're spoilt for choice when it comes to shopping.*

* *Brown Thomas is the home of the world's top designer labels with luxurious clothing, cosmetics and homeware departments – where you'll find the Pippa Collection! The restaurant on the top floor is the perfect spot to grab a bite to eat and take a little breather.*

* *Arnotts is the oldest and largest department store in Dublin, located on Henry Street. It has a lot of major brands covering clothing, homeware and the beauty hall is brilliant.*

* On the north side of the city is the **Jervis Shopping Centre** which has a great mix of high-street brands like Stradivarius and Bershka.

SEE

* No visit to Dublin is complete without a trip to the **Guinness Storehouse**. Take a tour with tastings and have a pint of the black stuff at their rooftop bar, which offers 360-degree view over the city.

* Take in all of the sights Dublin has to offer by getting on the **Hop On, Hop Off Tour** – from Kilmainham Gaol to Christ Church Cathedral. Go on a nice, sunny day and enjoy the views from the open-top bus.

* **Dublin Zoo** is a must-see experience in Dublin. It's located in the Phoenix Park and is the perfect day out for families, friends and couples.

* **The National Botanic Gardens** is such a beautiful place to explore. Situated in Glasnevin, entry to the gardens is free. It holds more than 15,000 plant species (300 of them endangered).

LONDON

London is one of my favourite destinations for a short break. It's so close to home, which means it's easy to get to and helps with the mammy guilt if you're leaving the kids. There's always something new to see and do in London and you can go back time and time again and not get everything done.

If it's your first time visiting, there are some things that you have to tick off your list. If you're with the girls you have to go shopping and that means you have to go to both Selfridges and Harrods. Selfridges has one of the most incredible shoe rooms you'll ever see; you could seriously spend hours there. Harrods is a stunning store, and even if you don't feel like spending a thousand pounds on a t-shirt you need to spend some time exploring. There is room after beautiful room of designer fashion and the beauty hall is out of this world. The staff on the counters are so knowledgeable and there are exclusive brands that you won't find anywhere else. You should time your visit to have lunch in the food hall. It's an incredible space, and you'll find food from all over the world in some amazing restaurants. I would recommend sitting down for a glass of champagne and watching the Knightsbridge locals do their food shop in what must be the most expensive supermarket in the world.

If you're in London around Christmas and have little ones to buy for, Selfridges and Harrods won't disappoint. You'll also want to visit Hamley's toy store on Regent Street, and while you're in that part of town I'd recommend nipping into Liberty just around the corner. Walk through the florist at the front of the store and be prepared to be wowed. Liberty is not only beautiful, it is also famous for its unusual brands and quirky collections. I'd make a beeline for the Christmas shop upstairs where you'll find beautiful decorations and brilliantly unusual gifts.

Once you've finished shopping, do something touristy. The London Eye might be cheesy but if it's a clear day the views are incredible. Do the Champagne Experience – you get fast-track entry, a host in the carriage and a glass of bubbly. It's a great way to see the sights. Another great way to get a bird's-eye view of London is by having brunch in a rooftop restaurant. You can't get a better view than from the Shard, the amazing glass building on the south side of the Thames near Borough Market. There are six bars and restaurants, all with phenomenal views.

Night-time in London is hard to beat and it seems like there's a new hotspot every week. Lots of the famous restaurants have bars that get pretty lively after dinner and you can choose from places like SUSHISAMBA, Chiltern Firehouse or Sexy Fish for a glamorous girls' night out. The Ned Hotel near Bank is a hotel, restaurant, bar and nightclub all rolled into one and you're guaranteed a good night there. I also love the Rosewood, which is the most beautiful hotel, not far from Oxford Street, with stunning rooms, a gorgeous bar, a great restaurant – and best of all, a resident dog in reception!

STAY

* *The Rosewood Hotel is my favourite hotel in London. It's a luxury five-star hotel located close to Covent Garden so you're in walking distance of all the main sights and shopping areas.*

* *The Ned is a really cool and trendy new hotel situated in the heart of London. Not only does it boast both an indoor and a rooftop pool, a gym and spa, it also has nine restaurants. It's become a favourite of lots of A-list celebrities too and it's no surprise why.*

* *Stylish and chic, Ham Yard Hotel in Soho is only a few minutes away from the hustle and bustle of Piccadilly Circus. Its bar has a great buzz and they serve the most delicious cocktails.*

* *The Hoxton, Shoreditch, is in an arty, fashionable and vibrant area of London full of trendy cafes and bars.*

EAT

* *Sexy Fish* is an Asian restaurant serving Japanese-inspired sushi, sashimi, fish and meat cooked on a robata grill. Live DJ sets, super-glam interiors and cocktails make this restaurant so special. It's perfect for a girls' night out.

* *Berners Tavern* is another place with incredible interiors. It's an upmarket British restaurant that serves the best steak.

* *La Bodega Negra* is a Mexican restaurant in Soho. It's a really fun place to go to with your friends on a night out. You can stay on late after dinner and have drinks – you need to try their Blackberry and Rosemary Margaritas.

* *Sketch London* in Mayfair, just off Oxford Street, is 'Instagram heaven'. The now world-renowned pink interiors in 'The Gallery' are a must-see. It's a lovely place to go for a late-night dinner or a champagne afternoon tea.

* *Bob Bob Ricard* in Soho has gone almost viral with its 'Press For Champagne' buttons. But the food here is also worth a mention, and it's a really nice treat for a date night.

* *EL&N cafe* is another place which is seriously Instagram-worthy. Not only is it visually pleasing and super-pretty, but the coffee and pastries are also lovely.

PARTY

* *Go to **The Ritz** for afternoon tea or a drink. It's a great old-school English experience.*

* *Madison*, the St Paul's rooftop terrace, is at its best in summertime. The rooftop offers stunning skyline views of London. There's always a great atmosphere here too with a brilliant DJ.

* *Radio Rooftop Bar* is another fab rooftop bar to go to for cocktails and tapas. Try to get here for sunset for the most gorgeous views of the city.

SHOP

* *King's Road* in Chelsea is lined with an eclectic mix of boutiques, designer stores and high-street favourites. It's the perfect place to go to if you want to find something special, with lots of great cafes perfect for a little shopping break.

* *Harrods* and *Selfridges* have all of the luxury brands you can think of, with amazing shoe and handbag departments. Their beauty halls are my favourite.

* *Oxford Street*, of course. It's home to the flagship Topshop store, which is amazing – I could actually spend hours there! Several of my other favourites like Zara, River Island and H&M are here too.

* *Liberty London* is just off Oxford Street and is another luxury department store. It's great to just have a walk around inside and browse. The beautiful flower display at the front door is also a must-see.

* *Covent Garden* in the West End is a really great place for shopping. One of its biggest draws has to be the Covent Garden Market – from Tuesday to Sunday lots of independent traders sell handcrafted items.

* *Camden Market* has over 1,000 shops and stalls selling fashion, music, art and food. If you want to find some vintage gems, this is the place to go.

SEE

* *The London Eye* is a must-do for amazing views. Not for anyone afraid of heights!

* No London trip is complete without a visit to **Madame Tussauds.** This waxwork museum is full of wax figures of some of the world's biggest stars. It's a fun place to go with the whole family.

* Go on a behind-the-scenes tour of the Harry Potter film studios at *Warner Bros. Studio Tour London* where you can see sets, costumes and props used in all of the Harry Potter films.

* *Hop On, Hop Off Tours* are a great way of seeing all of the sights and the most famous monuments London has to offer. Buy a 24-hour ticket and enjoy the freedom to hop on and off the buses and see the Tower of London, Buckingham Palace, Westminster Abbey, St Paul's Cathedral and Trafalgar Square, to name but a few.

PARIS

It would be really, really difficult to find a more romantic city than Paris. It is such a stunning place, with every street more beautiful than the last. But if you're tempted to pack tulle skirts, Breton tops and sky-high heels à la Carrie in *Sex and the City* then think again. What makes Paris so beautiful are the cobbled lanes of Montmartre, the winding streets of the Left Bank and the wide bridges that cross the Seine, and the only real way to see all of those is on foot. Sure, bring your favourite outfits for late-night dinners, but during the day a good boot or trainer is your friend as you walk from museum to café to cathedral to café, and on, and on. I find the best itinerary is one that visits all the essential tourist spots but leaves time for a coffee and croissant or glass of rosé in between each one.

Shopping in Paris is fantastic and you'll want to visit Galeries Lafayette to see how the Parisian women always look so chic, but what should be top of your list of priorities is a visit to a French pharmacy to see what gems you can pick up. Parisian chemists are full of brands we don't have here at home, and many are both potent and good value. Make-up artists used to pack suitcases full of **Bioderma Micellar Water** before it was available here, but now the brands to stock up on are Avibon and Embryolisse. Lots of French brands will have products that you can't buy here and which are worth checking out. It's a skincare fan's Aladdin's Cave.

My top tip is to ask your hotel concierge or receptionist for their favourite spots and recommendations – you'll find the best restaurants and time-saving secrets this way. Our concierge recommended getting a guide for the Eiffel Tower, which we weren't planning on doing, but it turned out to be brilliant. It's always worth listening to the locals.

Many people consider the Eiffel Tower a little touristy but there's no denying its beauty. The best place for pictures is from the Sacré-Cœur in Montmartre, both by day and at night when it is lit up from under the Bir-Hakeim bridge – this is the most stunning spot for a proposal if somebody needs a hint!

STAY

*   *Close to the Arc de Triomphe, Champs-Élysées and Trocadéro Gardens,* **The Peninsula** *is the ultimate in luxury. The Kardashians regularly frequent it during fashion weeks.*

*   *Another luxury hotel on Avenue George V, just off the Champs-Élysées, is the* **George V Four Seasons**. *From the moment you walk in, it's breathtaking. You can't miss the lavish floral display designed by Jeff Leatham – the arrangements are delivered to the hotel each week. This is a great place to drop in for a cocktail and do some people-watching and celebrity-spotting. Selena Gomez was sitting on the table next to us in the bar the last time I visited.*

*   **The Hoxton, Paris**, *is ultra-trendy and chic and definitely one to check out. Situated in a historic mansion in the 2nd arrondissement of Paris, this hotel is relatively new, having opened in 2017. Not only are the beds incredibly comfortable, the impeccably furnished lobby and outdoor courtyard are great areas to chill and people-watch.*

*   **Le Royal Monceau** *is the epitome of Parisian chic. With mirrored details at every corner, it has a fabulous spa and great bar. A stay here is the ultimate treat.*

EAT

*   *The four-storey* **Pink Mamma** *in the Pigalle neighbourhood is a must-do. If you like Italian food, you'll love it here.*

* *Favoured by many local Parisians,* **Pizzeria Popolare** *is a hidden gem that not many tourists know about. It serves delicious food and cocktails at affordable prices and has a brilliant atmosphere.*

* *Café Marly has a terrace which overlooks the glass pyramid of the Louvre – quite the location! Whether you come here for breakfast, lunch or dinner, the ambience is fantastic and the food is lovely.*

* *Restaurant Girafe is the place for you if you're a seafood lover. With unobstructed views of the Eiffel Tower, it's a stunning place to visit. As you can imagine, tables fill up very quickly so you're best to book a few weeks in advance.*

* *L'Oiseau Blanc at the Peninsula Hotel has stunning views of the city day and night. The restaurant offers typical French cuisine so if you've always wanted to try snails, here's your chance!*

PARTY

* *For an after-dinner cocktail, you need to visit* **Le Bar** *in the George V Hotel. Soaking in the grand interiors and atmosphere is totally worth it.*

* *Maison Sauvage is located in the Saint-Germain area which has a relaxed vibe. It's great for wine or cocktails and you can order food here also. It's a quaint, typically Parisian spot.*

* *Jacques' Bar at The Hoxton, Paris is an intimate cocktail bar with cosy interiors. Lovely for a romantic nightcap.*

SHOP

* *The Champs-Élysées is probably one of the most famous streets in the world. This tree-lined avenue has stores like Sephora and Abercrombie as well as designer labels such as Louis Vuitton.*

* *Galeries Lafayette is a high-end French department store full of lots of luxury fashion and beauty brands. Their beauty hall on the ground floor is heaven for any beauty lover.*

* *For a real Parisian experience you should visit the famous flea market at Porte de Clignancourt. Its official name is Les Puces de Saint-Ouen but all the locals call it Les Puces, which means The Fleas. It's open every Saturday and Sunday and it's a great way to spend a morning. Get a coffee and wander around for a few hours – and you'll need time, it's the biggest antique market in the world and it can get more than 120,000 visitors each weekend!*

SEE

* *You can't miss the **Louvre Museum** and your chance to see the Mona Lisa in the flesh, as well as many other world-famous pieces of art.*

* *Were you even in Paris if you didn't see the **Eiffel Tower**? You can get tickets to go up to the very top and take in the views. Head across the road to Place du Trocadéro for the perfect photo opp with the Eiffel Tower in the background.*

* *Take a cruise down the **River Seine** for a completely different view of the city.*

* *The **Arc de Triomphe** is one of the most famous monuments in Paris. Lots of people don't know that you can actually go up to the very top and take in the views from there.*

NEW YORK

I love New York. It's one of my favourite cities in the world. Perfect for a getaway with Brian or for a long weekend with friends – you can't get tired of this ever-changing city. Whether it's your first time or your tenth time, there's something so magical about standing on Broadway with Times Square in one direction and downtown in the other.

Like Paris, New York is a great city to see by foot, but it's immense so you're better off doing it a bit at a time, picking a neighbourhood and exploring it before moving on. Spend a morning uptown and do a little shopping on Fifth Avenue before heading over to Times Square for some touristy photos. An afternoon wandering around the boutiques in the West Village, with a stop for lunch or a cocktail, will make you feel like you're in a different city. Then take a wander down Broadway in SoHo before ducking into Little Italy for a pizza slice or cannoli before you walk down Mulberry Street and watch as Italy turns into Chinatown. Then hop on a subway and go the whole way uptown to enjoy a picnic in Central Park with the backdrop of the city behind you.

There's a lot to do before you even think about going down to see the financial district where you should really visit the 9/11 memorial. It is moving and heartbreaking, but positioned between the rebuilt skyscrapers it really demonstrates the resilience of New Yorkers.

Shopping and eating are two of Manhattan's biggest draws and you'll want to visit Macy's (for its sheer size), Bloomingdales (for its designer brands) and Woodbury Common (for discounted designer deals about an hour out of the city). Remember to bring your passport to the visitor centre in Macy's to collect your savings pass that will give you 10 per cent off!

STAY

* *The Soho Grand Hotel has a really cool retro vibe in a great downtown location. There's an excellent restaurant, bar and nightclub in the hotel so you don't really have to leave.*

* *If you can forget about the owner for a second, The Dominick (previously called the Trump SoHo) is a great hotel. It has fabulous interiors and good-sized rooms – most hotel rooms in NYC are pretty small.*

* *The Sofitel combines French luxury with American spirit in a great midtown location between Times Square and Broadway.*

* *A great place to stay for a little bit of home on your holidays is Fitzpatrick Grand Central. There are good-sized rooms, it's in a great location and has a lively bar!*

* *NoMo is a hidden gem in SoHo. There is a nice bar and restaurant and you're mere steps away from some great shopping.*

EAT

* *TAO, Downtown is a cool, fun, buzzy Asian restaurant with unbelievable interiors! Go for dinner and stay late at the bar.*

* *Beauty & Essex in the Lower East Side is found at the back of a pawn shop. The best bit? They serve free champagne in the ladies' toilets!*

* *Another great Asian restaurant is Buddakan. You might recognize this one from an episode of Sex and the City and it still feels like somewhere you might spot Carrie.*

* *The Standard Grill is in the famous Standard Hotel in the Meatpacking District. Great American food and a really cool crowd.*

* *New York is famous for brunch and some of my favourites are: Sarabeth's (order my favourite pancakes and bacon), Balthazar, Jack's Wife Freda and The Butcher's Daughter for any veggies visiting the city.*

* *You'll need to stop off for treats and if I were you I'd go to the famous Magnolia Bakery for cupcakes or to the Dominique Ansel Bakery where you'll get the original cronuts – be warned though, they sell out early!*

* *I'd also make time to go to Serendipity 3 where you have to order the world-famous frozen hot chocolate. Oh. My. God. It's so good.*

Tip – restaurants should be booked in advance of trip to avoid disappointment. The best ones book up early. I use the Open Table app for bookings as it is handy and convenient. Bookings can be made thirty days in advance.

PARTY

* *Head to the Westlight rooftop bar in the William Vale Hotel in Brooklyn for fantastic views of the Manhattan skyline.*

* *The St Cloud Bar on the rooftop of The Knickerbocker Hotel off Times Square has a chilled-out vibe and is an oasis in the middle of bustling Times Square.*

* *Go to 230 Fifth for a brilliant rooftop experience and fab cocktails. You can book a spot for drinks on Open Table.*

* *The Dead Rabbit on Water Street is an Irish Bar but not as we know it. Downstairs is the Tap Room where you'll find after-work Wall Street types letting off steam; upstairs are award-winning cocktails in The Parlor; and some of New York's coolest parties are held in **The Occasional** on the top floor.*

* *For a night to remember head to **Please Don't Tell** on St Marks Place. You're actually looking for a hot-dog joint called Crif Dogs and when you're there you'll see a phone booth at the back. Pick up the phone, press the buzzer once and you'll be admitted into the coolest, tiniest cocktail bar ever!*

SHOP

* *It's good to remember that UK high-street stores, like Zara, Topshop and H&M, are usually priced higher in the US.*

* *Outlet stores, like **Woodbury Common**, are good for discounted bargains, and are located a bus ride outside of the city. They're especially good for kids' and men's clothing and footwear.*

* *SoHo is great for a mix of boutiques and high-street shopping.*

* *Barneys is Carrie Bradshaw's dream and is a smaller department store with a good mix of contemporary designers, make-up and beauty.*

* *Go to **Times Square** for giant Disney, M&Ms and MAC stores. You can also pick up touristy bits here and if you're in the mood for a mid-shop cocktail, The Marriott has a rotating bar with brilliant views of the madness below.*

* *Fifth Avenue* has all the flagship stores and is amazing for window shopping. The famous Tiffany's is here – bring a croissant in your handbag and say you had breakfast here!

* Shopping in New York wouldn't be complete without a trip to *Sephora*. I love trying the brands exclusive to the USA and testing the limits of my baggage allowance with all my purchases.

SEE

* Everyone tells you to go to the top of the Empire State Building but my tip is to head straight for the **Top of the Rock at the Rockefeller Centre**. The view is unbelievable and has the added bonus of including the Empire State Building so you get better photos!

* Take a picnic and relax in **Central Park**, an oasis of green in the middle of New York's high-speed lifestyle. The zoo there is great if you have small children with you. For refreshment visit the **Loeb Boathouse** with its incredible lakeside location in the middle of the park.

* The **One World Trade Center**, which replaced the twin towers of the old WTC, is the tallest building in New York, and you can take a tour and head to the very top. It's also right by Ground Zero, the incredibly moving monument to the victims of 9/11.

* **Times Square** is, of course, a must, and really encapsulates the hustle and bustle of New York City.

* Take a trip out on the water to see the **Statue of Liberty**. You can get a boat to Liberty Island and take the tour – I recommend booking your tickets in advance to skip the long queues! Or you can take the Staten Island ferry – while it won't land on Liberty Island the ferry is free and offers spectacular views of the Statue.

DUBAI

The same flight length away as New York but in the other direction is Dubai. It might not be top of your list to visit but it should be. It's a great destination for a five-day break with friends (it has a manageable four-hour time difference) or for a sunny holiday with family – and the one thing that everyone will say about Dubai is that there's loads to do there.

The choice of places to stay can be overwhelming. There are the resorts on the Palm Islands, which are beautiful, or there are stunning options at Dubai Marina or downtown, which is where you'll find a lot of the nightlife.

Choose your time of year carefully. It gets blisteringly hot in Dubai so you might not want to visit from May to September when it is a minimum of about thirty-eight degrees. On really hot days you might want to head to one of the malls. This might not sound like fun for anyone but a shopaholic, but there's so much more to the malls than shopping. They're more like theme parks and you'll find rides, ice rinks, aquariums, giant cinemas and even ski slopes! Ollie loved the aquarium in The Dubai Mall and shows everyone the photo of him swimming with the penguins (spoiler: it's a camera trick).

The food in Dubai is unreal – from international restaurants in the hotels to local food in the souks of Dubai Creek, there really is something for everyone. One of the most popular things to do is a Friday brunch. The working week runs from Sunday to Thursday in Dubai so for the locals Friday is their equivalent to our Saturday, and brunch is big business. In lots of places you pay a flat entry fee and then eat and drink to your heart's content. The food is amazing, the drinks are flowing and there is often a DJ or party vibe. If you're there with friends find one by a pool for a great way to spend the day.

Everyone thinks Dubai is brand new and made out of steel and glass, but that's not quite true. Dubai Creek is the old heart of the city and the markets there are really interesting, or you can take a tour of the Jumeirah Mosque. If you like a bit of action you can head out of the city and go dune buggying, camel riding or even stay in a traditional Bedouin camp!

STAY

* *The Ritz-Carlton* has an enviable location along the JBR Walk (in Jumeirah Beach Resort). It combines luxury surroundings with an Emirati experience.

* *The Anantara* is located on The Palm. It's highly recommended for families, has good facilities and a choice of restaurants and pools. There are children's activity clubs available.

* *The Palace Downtown* is a great hotel with incredible views of the Burj Khalifa. It's really close to the Dubai Mall so is ideal if you're on a shopping trip.

* *The Al Qasr Hotel* is designed like a Middle Eastern summer palace and has a mile-long beach, a beautiful spa and an enormous pool. Perfect for a relaxing break.

EAT

* *Souk Madinat Jumeirah*, a traditional Middle Eastern covered bazaar, is a great dining spot with a vast range of restaurants on a waterside setting.

* *Fish Beach Taverna* at Le Meridien Mina Seyahi serves delicious Turkish and Greek cuisine. My top tip is to request a table on the beach so the kids can play on the sand.

* *PLAY Restaurant & Lounge* is located on the thirty-sixth floor of the H Hotel and serves Asian fusion food. It has a luxurious interior, live music and a DJ.

* *Pier 7* is located at the Dubai Marina and you can choose from seven different restaurants, one on each storey, each offering a different 'lifestyle dining' experience.

* *At.mosphere Restaurant* is the world's tallest restaurant at 442 metres from the ground! It's located in the Burj Khalifa, the tallest building in the world, and is a once in a lifetime kind of experience.

PARTY

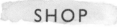

* *Soho Garden* is set on the Meydan Racecourse in downtown Dubai and has a vibrant mix of music, food and cocktails.

* You have to experience a party brunch when you're in Dubai and one of the best is at **Wet Deck** in the W Hotel at The Palm. It has a brunch buffet, club DJ and a swim-up bar! The food is unreal and the cocktails are delicious. It runs from 1pm to 5pm every Friday.

SHOP

* **The Mall of the Emirates** has every brand and designer all under one roof. There are good restaurants, kids' activity zones, ice skating and skiing!

* For a more authentic Middle Eastern shopping experience you should head to the souks for beautiful gold jewellery, exotic spices and traditional oud perfumes.

SEE

*   *For something really different I recommend a visit to **Dubai Garden Glow**, the world's largest glow-in-the-dark garden made up of millions of energy-saving bulbs (it's great to visit in the early evening).*

*   *If you're travelling with a mini Jurassic enthusiast, **Dino Park** has more than 120 animatronic dinosaurs on display.*

*   *Get out of the city for the day and try some more adrenaline-fuelled activities like camel trekking (watch out, they spit!), dune buggying and sand surfing. You can stay at Bedouin camps and eat under the stars for a memorable trip within your trip. Be warned though, they love to get the tourists up for a mortifying belly dance!*

'The beauty of Dubai is that it has something for everyone.'

THE ALGARVE, PORTUGAL

It's hard not to love Portugal for a family holiday and if you're travelling with your little ones for the first time the Algarve is a great option. It really is the perfect family holiday destination – the temperature in the Algarve is great for a young family, everyone is so welcoming and most resorts have all the baby supplies you'll need on hand so there's no need to cart everything including the kitchen sink over with you. There are usually kids' clubs and entertainment, which is important when you have boys with as much energy as mine, and the menus are always perfect for parents and kids alike.

One of the best things about a trip here is the short flight time, especially if you're nervous about things like that. It's just under three hours so with the right amount of snacks, toys and bribery it's over before you know it.

We've been a number of times now and really love Quinta do Lago for a break with the boys. We've also been to a Martinhal resort in Sagres which is brilliant for anyone with kids – they have supervised play areas that allow parents to have a meal while the children are occupied. Genius!

The Algarve is the perfect spot for a relaxing sun holiday where you don't want to do too much, but if lying by the pool gets a bit boring there are plenty of other options. Car hire is easy and the roads are good so getting out and exploring for a day or two is a great way to spend your time. There are pretty fishing villages to explore, traditional mountain villages to visit, or if you're feeling more adventurous the stunning Spanish city of Seville is just a two-hour drive from Quinta do Lago and makes a lovely day trip if you're on a two-week break.

STAY

* *The Conrad Hotel* in Quinta do Lago is absolutely stunning. The golf course runs right to the water, the spa is world class and there's a brilliant kids' club.

* *We've rented villas in* **Quinta do Lago** *too, which can be a great holiday option if you've a group of friends or lots of family staying together.*

EAT

* *Bovino Steakhouse* in Quinta do Lago has an amazing setting and delicious food. There's a supervised kids' area, face painting and a bouncy castle. There's live music too and it's great for all the family.

* *Parrilla Natural* is probably our favourite restaurant in Portugal. It's close by in Almancil and has the most beautiful outdoor setting.

* *The Shack* is right on the water in Quinta do Lago and is great for a casual bite.

* *Another family-friendly restaurant is* **Casa do Lago**. *The food is great and there's a pool on site!*

* *Maria's* on the beach serves the best prawn curry I've ever had. There's live music every day and it's great fun.

* *If you're in need of something healthy I love* **Pure Boutique Café**, *they do fantastic breakfasts.*

SHOP

* I tend not to shop much on a family holiday but there's a small mall at the entry to Quinta do Lago that has cute boutiques if you need a fix.

* There's a farmer's market held in Quinta do Lago once a month that has lots of traditional produce and is well worth checking out.

* If you're in need of a proper shopping fix the MAR *shopping centre* is less than a fifteen-minute drive away and has all the shops you want including Sephora and Zara Home – just be careful with your baggage allowance!

SEE

* You may not want to leave the resort but if you hire a car there are lots of beautiful coastal fishing towns to visit and you can get to *Sagres*, almost at the most westerly tip of the Algarve, in about an hour and fifteen minutes. The views from the lighthouse are stunning and Sagres itself is a lovely fishing town.

* Quinta do Lago is probably best known as a golf resort so if you or your partner like to play then this is a great holiday destination for you. If it's your partner that plays I recommend letting them play early in the morning and then swapping childcare duties for the afternoon while you head for a nap or to the spa! Everyone's a winner.

PART SIX

Well-being

CHAPTER SIXTEEN

What I Know Now

FRIENDSHIP

I consider myself quite private. It might not seem that way when you follow me on a couple of different social media platforms – but I am. I mean, I put a lot out there, but it's on my terms. I have a very tight-knit group of people both in and out of work. I've always been like that and I have the same main group of friends that I've had since I was twelve. I have been known to say 'Don't trust people who don't have old friends', which might sound extreme, but I can't help wondering, 'What happened? Where are the people from their past?' I obviously have a very active imagination!

What I love about my oldest friends is that, because we've been a group for so long, everyone does something different. One is a Montessori teacher, one's a solicitor, there's a food and beverage operations manager, all sorts of things. I think that mix is so important, it gives you a perspective on life. When we're together we just talk about normal things and husbands and kids. Because we know each other so well, we know all sorts of stories about each other, so a night out is always really funny. I don't get to see them as much as I'd like because everyone is so busy and two of them live in the UK now, but they're still the people I rely on when something bad happens. They're the ones I call. And friendship like that is priceless.

As well as the girls, Brian and Susanna, I have my other Brian – Brian Dowling. We met when I did panto in 2009. That's ten years ago now – where has a decade gone? I was the fairy, and he was the ugly sister, obviously! Although Brian says it should have been the other way around! We just clicked straight away, he's a tonic and a half. You know when you have that friend that you just laugh with constantly? He's that for me, he absolutely cracks me up. We know each other's personalities so well and we know how to take the mickey out of each other – which you might see on my Instagram whenever he's around. He lives in LA now, but he's always been really supportive of me and comes home a lot to be at my events. He loves a party, and he knows I love to throw one. We're two lushes! His husband, Arthur, works in LA and

Brian decided to make the move to be with him. He's far from home but he's destined for big things out there. I can't wait to see what he does.

Sadly, Brian lost his mum, Rosie, not long ago. She was the same age as my mum when she passed away and it was sudden. It was so weird how that happened to both of us and it was only when his mum died that he said to me, 'You think you know what someone is going through, but until it happens to you, you have no idea.' It has brought us even closer together which is really lovely, but it's bittersweet.

Take care of your friends, and they will take care of you.

WHAT PEOPLE DON'T KNOW ABOUT ME

Because I work so much, I want it to be fun and I want it to be exciting. I think people might think I'm more serious than I am, but it's important to have a good time too. I'm always laughing. I'm pretty sarcastic and I don't think people expect that – people are often surprised by my sense of humour! I think people see it occasionally on social media when Brian Dowling is around because he brings out the messer in me, but I'm actually like that most of the time!

LOSING MY MUM

When I was thirty, my mum passed away very suddenly. She was only sixty-one. It was such a shock and the timing of everything was so weird. Up until then I was still scrambling to put things together and figure it all out and when she passed, work was just starting to go really well and get busy. I think that it gave me a massive kick and an urge to be really good at what I was doing. Honestly, it reminded me that life is so short and showed me that things can literally change in one day. I've always been very relaxed, a real 'don't worry it will be fine' person, but now this really hit home for me. I know how superficial things are, and that if someone says something bad about me, or something doesn't go to plan at work, it just doesn't matter in the grand scheme of things. I carry that attitude with me all the time now. I'm very driven and passionate about everything that I'm doing, but if something doesn't go right I just think 'it's fine', it's not the be-all and end-all.

Things were only just starting to take off for me when Mum died, and my first Fashion Factory was due to take place just two weeks after she passed. I didn't think I could do it and asked Brian and Susanna to refund the people that had booked. In my mind I was definitely cancelling it, or at the very least postponing it. Then I spoke to a friend and they told me that they didn't think I'd feel that much better in a few weeks – or even months – and that really resonated with me. The Fashion Factory was something I wanted, my own thing, not a job for someone else, something that I had been so excited about. I decided to go ahead and do it.

I was thinking of Mum the whole time that day. She would have loved it. She was so glam and she would have been in her element with the nice hotel, afternoon tea, talking fashion and beauty. She would have absolutely loved the day and that's why I did it.

Deciding to do it was the easy part – but once I was up on stage I was terrified. I felt like I did a bad job, if I'm honest. Brian, Susanna, Tara and Niamh were there. Niamh looked after the fashion show that day and handled the models and clothes and I did the rest, but it's just a blur. A lot of the months after that were a blur. It's hard to explain, but I think before if I heard that someone's mum or dad had died I thought it was very sad, but until you go through it you have no idea how hard it is.

Everyone expects to lose a parent at some stage, but when they're young and it's sudden, it's very hard. I think now I would tell anyone going through it to be easy on themselves and to accept all offers of help. Ollie was only one and I definitely still thought of myself as a new mum, trying to figure it all out. I relied on Brian more than ever. He picked up all the slack at home, and with Ollie. When I actually think of it now I realize I've forgotten months of it. I had Susanna, too, of course. We were living close by and we were such a support to each other. I'm so thankful I have a sister. I love my brother too, but it's a different bond with a sister.

I learned a lot from Mum's passing. It gave me such a drive to do things and not put things on the long finger. You shouldn't be afraid to fail at something or to put yourself out there. What's the worst that could happen? You can't be a scaredy cat. What are you waiting for?

Now, five years on, the things that hit me hardest are the happy things. I think you're prepared for the anniversaries and occasions like Christmas or her birthday, you've worked yourself up to them, but when something amazing happens unexpectedly that's when it gets me. You feel sad for yourself. The boys don't know any different, but I'm sad for them that she's not around when the happy things happen. When something really cool happens or business is great I think, it's not fair that she's not here for that. That's what's really hard.

'It reminded me that life is so short and showed me that things can literally change in one day.'

CHAPTER SEVENTEEN

Becoming a Mum

What have I learned since becoming a mum? Well you don't need as much sleep as you think, that's for sure! But really, it just changes your whole everything. You realize that it's your most important job, first and foremost – everything after that is a bonus. You want your kids to be happy and healthy, and they just put things into perspective. Every little milestone they get to is amazing. Becoming a mum changes absolutely everything.

I found going from one to two okay. I felt more capable the second time round, plus it wasn't as much of a shock to the system – when Ollie was born he was huge! He was two weeks early and over nine pounds. He was just massive and I had him by section.

I had gestational diabetes and they told me he was growing at an alarming rate – not really something you want to hear! The GD meant that I was on a really strict diet, which was awful, and I had to prick myself and check my sugar levels four times a day. I was like a demon because I have such a sweet tooth. I just hated it.

I ended up having him two weeks early, my big boy, and he wouldn't stop feeding. I was breastfeeding, obviously for the first time, and I thought there was something wrong with him. I brought him back to the hospital after three weeks and said, 'There's something really wrong with him, you need to test him for something because he won't stop. It takes me an hour to feed him and then I get maybe fifteen minutes and then he wants more.' I remember being so emotional, I just couldn't understand it. The nurse looked at me and said, 'He's grand, he's a baby, you're fine and he's getting plenty of food. Off you go.' I remember leaving feeling so dejected. I had been expecting more than that. I wanted her to sympathize and tell me it wasn't normal and that he was a savage, but I got nothing.

I remember friends of mine breastfeeding their babies and they'd do ten minutes on one boob, ten minutes on the other, and then the baby would go into the pram for an hour and a half. And there we were, pinned to a chair for days. I remember one shocked friend saying to me, 'You've been feeding him for an hour!' I was like I know, this is how we roll. That's why I have nothing in the boob department now. He took it all!

Then I had Louis and although he was the same it seemed a bit easier. Maybe because I was expecting it after Ollie or because I was just used to it at that stage, but it wasn't as much of an emotional turmoil. I just had really hungry boys!

After a while with Ollie I got into my groove, and a few months in I introduced a bottle as well as breastfeeding. You have to do what's right for you at the time and try not to be hard on yourself. I hate all the emotions and guilt that you feel as a new mother. You think you're the worst mother in the world if you give a bottle as well as the breast, or if you just give a bottle, but, really, why can't we all just be kinder to ourselves? Not only do you have other feckers judging you, but you're also judging yourself and that's not great. And you know what, my boys are six and three now, and they're totally fine.

Speaking of babies, one of the most popular posts on Pippa.ie over the years has been the one about packing my hospital bag for the birth of the boys. So here it is if you need some inspiration. And if you're in the middle of packing – congratulations and good luck!

WHAT'S IN MY HOSPITAL BAG

let's start with baby

* *Delivery outfit* (baby receiving gown/hat/vest). I got mine from an American website called babybeminematernity.com, but you can pick something cute from your favourite brand.

* *Five vests* in newborn size. I had some from Mothercare and Dunnes.

* *Five Babygros* in newborn size or 0–3 months. I packed ones from Primark and Next. When I was having Louis I packed some that Ollie had worn so they'd be in the same Babygro in photos.

* *Two pairs of mittens and two hats.* Mine were from Mothercare.

* *Two tiny cardigans.*

* *One or two cellular blankets.* The hospital will wrap the baby in their own ones but you'll probably want to use your own when you get up to your bed.

* *Muslin cloths* for feeding and cleaning up. A good handful of them!

* *Newborn nappies/cotton wool/Water Wipes.*

Tips

* *Personally, I like to wash the baby clothes before I use them. I wash them using Fairy Non-Bio.*

* *I only buy a handful of newborn sizes. These really don't last long (unfortunately!), as the baby grows out of these tiny sizes in only a couple of weeks. I'm going by Ollie here – he was nine pounds and never lost an ounce, just kept gaining! I'd recommend very few items in newborn size until you know what weight your baby is. Everything else I bought was in sizes 0–3 months.*

* *My top tip is to pack your baby outfits into food bags or ziplock bags and label them. Include a vest, Babygro, hat and nappy in each one. This way you, or whoever is with you, won't have to search for anything – it'll be easy to put your hands on the food bags.*

For me

* *Gownie. This is a hospital gown I bought on Baby Be Mine Maternity, the website I mentioned above. They do really cute matching items for mum and baby. I bought a delivery gown, which is the exact same as the one the hospital would provide you with. It's grey with white polka dots. (Susanna thought I was gas even thinking of this! I loved it though.)*

* *PJs. I kept with a navy theme so I could mix and match bottoms and tops. Opting for darker colours is a good idea – I wouldn't recommend white PJs for your hospital stay! I got mine from Primark, the material is really light and they're loose fitting. Don't buy cosy fleecy PJs – maternity wards are hot. All of the Primark pj tops or nightdresses are easily pulled down, which is something you want to keep in mind when you're buying yours if you think you*

might be breastfeeding. Even if you're not breastfeeding, they're still a good idea for skin-to-skin with your baby.

*   I also packed a **cosy pair of socks**, a pair of slippers and a light knee-length navy dressing gown.

*   Two nursing bras (nude and black). I got both of mine from ASOS.

*   Granny knickers/Bridget Jones knickers (whatever you want to call them!). Get the cheap multipacks in either Primark or Dunnes – I wouldn't spend any more than you have to on them as you'll want to burn them afterwards! Get high leg ones, not mini briefs as they'll sit too low, which is not ideal if you've had a C-section.

*   Maternity pads (I went Boots own brand).

*   Breast pads (Lansinoh).

*   Nipple cream (Lansinoh). This was such a lifesaver around day three or four. I remember the agony – but this cream was excellent and really helped.

*   Nipple shields (Boots own brand).

*   Multi-Mam compress pads. You can cut them in half to make them last longer and they're really good if you keep them in the fridge.

*   Towel (dark colour).

*   Mini hairdryer/brushes/hair turban (this is neater than bringing a second towel, I bought one in Boots). Hair bobbin and dry shampoo (if you don't want to wash your hair).

* *Shampoo/conditioner/body lotion/hand cream/face serum/eye cream/moisturizer/lip oil.* I packed lots of minis. Bring whatever gives you a bit of comfort and whatever will make you feel good afterwards. That first shower is bliss. Bring it if it'll perk you up.

* **Essential toiletries** like toothpaste/toothbrush/deodorant.

* My **make-up bag** for hospital was the smallest I've ever packed! I just brought a palette and mascara, concealer and nude lip gloss. You're not really thinking about make-up.

* **Nursing pillow.** It's brilliant for supporting baby and your back while bottle or breastfeeding.

* **Going home outfit.** Make it comfy!

Extras:

* **A spare top** for hubby!

* **Phone charger/camera.**

* **Small pressie** for Ollie from Louis. It was such a nice idea, and he was delighted to get a pressie from the baby in the hospital when he came to visit.

* **Car seat** – you can't go home without it!

CHAPTER EIGHTEEN

The Power
of Positivity

I think the power of the mind is everything. It's incredibly important. It's so easy to be negative, and sometimes you might be in a negative space without even realizing. A lot of us can lean towards that behaviour and it might just be the way you are, but I think that once you acknowledge it and objectively observe how you're acting then you can re-programme your mind.

I wasn't always this positive, I taught myself to be this way. I read books on positive thinking and watch documentaries. I don't take everything they say as gospel, but I take bits from everything I read or listen to and apply it to my daily life. I'm really into podcasts and audiobooks at the moment. They're great because I don't always have the time to sit down and read so I'll listen to them in the car or when we're on holiday.

I believe everyone should be listening to something or reading something positive because in this world it's very easy to get bogged down and become negative. It's easy to look at someone's life and say 'if only that were me', or 'isn't it nice for some'. Well no, it's not. I've fallen into this trap myself. But actually, I think anyone can do anything they want to do. I really believe that.

People are held back from pursuing their dreams because they're afraid they'll be judged or afraid that they'll fail – and some people even think that they don't deserve good things. But I remember being told that everyone else is too busy focusing on their own lives to really notice you, so you may as well give things a try. I know that not everyone wants to do what I'm doing and be a business owner or work for themselves, but everyone has their own dreams to pursue, and everyone can try to embrace a positive and happy attitude in whatever they are doing in life.

JUST BE NICE

I always try to be in a good mood. I'm such a believer in being nice to people and being kind to them. You don't know what people are going through. Whether you're in a cafe buying a coffee in the morning or in the office working with your team, you have to remember that you don't know what's going on in other people's lives. I'm always very conscious of others and try to be compassionate when someone is being difficult, because I don't know what's happened at home that morning or that week. Being nice makes you feel better too and when you go around being nice to people they tend to return the favour.

That's part of the reason why I don't understand why some people would be horrible online and try to bring other people down. You're only really bringing yourself down by doing that, it's a vicious circle.

Brian is a pretty positive person too and we've probably rubbed off on each other over the years. I try to see the good in every situation and say 'Things could be worse, this isn't the end of the world'. A couple of years ago I read *The Secret* which taught me to always practise gratitude. No matter what you have in life, once you are grateful for it, it manifests even more. 100 per cent. I have *The Secret* app on my phone and you've probably seen me post some of the daily reminders on Instagram.

Every night before bed, I write down what I'm grateful for. I feel so lucky I have a roof over my head, I feel so lucky my kids are healthy and asleep next door. I do it with the boys too. Sometimes I'm sure they think I'm mad, but they don't know any different. I ask them every day what their favourite part of the day was, and when they tell me, I say, 'Do you know how lucky you are? Why are you so lucky?' I'm always trying to get them to think about nice things that have happened so that they are aware of how lucky they are. Hopefully it will become a habit that they grow up with and my positivity will become theirs too.

Inspiring Women that will make you think

Michelle Obama

If you haven't read her book, *Becoming* (or listened to the audio version), you need to get on it immediately. She's powerfully positive and is such a force for good in everything she does.

Oprah Winfrey

I love listening to Oprah. Her podcast *SuperSoul Conversations* is designed to guide you through life's big questions and help you become the best version of yourself. There are interviews with authors, wellness experts and thought leaders who share their expertise on living your best, most positive life.

Georgie Crawford

Following her breast cancer journey, broadcaster Georgie Crawford started her podcast *The Good Glow* to encourage us to prioritize ourselves and inspire positive change. Each episode sees Georgie interview well-known people about their own wellness journey and opens up the conversation around self-care. I really love it and was honoured when she asked me to record an episode.

Jenny Taaffe

My friend and business mentor Jenny is an incredible woman. After being diagnosed with pancreatic cancer and receiving a terminal prognosis in August 2018 Jenny has literally beaten all the odds. Her positivity in the face of a seemingly desperate situation has inspired me every day and I really believe that positivity has inspired thousands of others too.

ME TIME

How often do you take some time to do something just for you? We're all so busy working or with our kids or studying, that we don't feel that we have the time to be good to ourselves. We feel embarrassed saying we're getting our nails done, or we're going to a spa for a day. We try and justify it or make excuses, but it's so important to look after ourselves. Whether it's a yoga class, or a nail appointment, or a walk with a friend, I think we need to schedule those things in. Plan ahead. Plan that girly night away, or time with your husband. Book that nail appointment and put your weekly walk with your friend into your diary so you can't cancel it.

If you don't make the time then life gets in the way. You get home and you're busy with dinner or with uniforms and the night goes and you're getting up and doing it all over again and it becomes a cycle. If we have twenty-four hours in the day, what's an hour out of that? You're probably spending it scrolling through social media anyway. Instead of doing that put your headphones in and go for a walk. Listen to music or, if you're like me, listen to an audiobook or podcast, something uplifting. At the moment, Oprah Winfrey's podcasts and Michelle Obama's audiobook are keeping me company on my walks. Michelle Obama is so articulate and her voice is really soothing (she reads her own audiobook). She has a very powerful positivity.

If we don't make time for ourselves we will inevitably get burnt out. I know if I'm exhausted or feeling stressed I'll get narky with Brian or the kids, I won't be able to concentrate on anything and I know it's time to press pause and look after myself. We should all be doing it.

Self-Care Sunday

Everyone needs some time alone, here are some quick ideas for your end of week 'me time'.

1. **Have a bath.** *Tell everyone you're having 30/40/60 minutes to yourself and run a bath. Light a candle (from the Pippa Collection!), grab your book or your tablet (put it somewhere safe!) and lie back and enjoy some quality me time.*

2. **Put on a face mask,** *close your bedroom door and lie down for fifteen minutes on your own. In a busy world, this can sometimes feel like a mini break.*

3. **Go for a walk.** *Whether it's on your own or with a podcast for company or a friend in tow, some time in the fresh air will do you the world of good.*

4. **Go for a drive.** *If you have a small baby it can be hard to get any time on your own, but if they like to sleep in the car a drive can be the perfect answer. Put on some good music or an audiobook and head for the open road while they nap and you listen to something good.*

5. **Join a book club.** *It's a great excuse to start reading and an even better excuse to get together with some friends. Everyone needs a hobby and a night with the girls. If there isn't one to join, set one up! If the pressure of hosting is too much, agree to have it in a local cafe or hotel once a month so you don't even have to do the dusting!*

PART SEVEN

·───────────✵───────────·

All About

Me

CHAPTER NINETEEN

The Fast Answers to my Most-Asked Questions

How old are you?

I'm thirty-five. I was born on 7 August 1984. All ten pounds eleven ounces of me!

How long have you and Brian been together?

We met in January 2008. Nearly twelve years ago!

Where do you live?

County Kildare. Back to my roots and we love it.

What's your favourite holiday destination?

Either Portugal or Dubai.

What are your favourite shops in Dublin?

I love Brown Thomas, it's fashion and make-up heaven. Plus, my candle collection is stocked there so I love walking in to look at them. I always feel so proud and wonder if it's all real! I love Loulerie on Chatham Street too, it's a beautiful jewellery shop.

Who does your hair?

I go to Peter Mark in Stephen's Green. Tracey Rafter is fab!

Do you have extensions?

I have been getting the **Raptures** for about two years now, they're like fillers for the hair. I love them, I'd say I'm addicted! Tracey applies them in minutes, they're easy to maintain and there's been no damage to my own hair.

What's your favourite lipstick?

Oh, that's so hard! Probably **Tom Ford Spanish Pink** or **Bad Lieutenant**. Both are nude. I love a great nude lipstick. They're so luxurious. **MAC Peach Blossom** or **Shanghai Spice** are beautiful too.

What's your favourite foundation?

NARS Sheer Glow, or any of the NARS ones to be honest. They are stunning! My latest find that I love is the **Your Skin But Better CC cream by IT Cosmetics,** it has decent coverage and it contains SPF 50.

What's the colour on the walls in your hall?

This is probably my most-asked question! It's by Colourtrend and the shade is Silver Moonlight. I'm so happy with it.

Where is the floor from in your hall?

It's from the Design Emporium in Dublin. It's an engineered oak chevron floor.

How tall are you?

I'm five foot nine. People always say 'Oh you're taller than I expected' when they meet me.

What size do you wear in POCOs?

An eight regular in every style.

How are you always so happy?

I've probably trained my mind to be that way. I read a lot of books that focus on happiness and positivity. I love *The Secret* and live by it. It works! It's important to be grateful for everything you have – and I don't just mean big things. Be grateful every day for all the little things, it makes you appreciate life more and in turn makes you happy.

What's your favourite tan?

Probably **Tan Luxe**. Their tan drops for the face have been my best find. They're amazing.

How do you keep fit?

I'm not at all fit. This is something I'm working on, slowly!

Do you get stressed?

I do – but I probably wouldn't portray it (which isn't always a good thing). My husband knows when I'm stressed. When I find myself like that I usually take a big step back to refocus and calm down. When it comes to work though, nothing is worth getting stressed over. Your health is the most important thing.

Will you open a permanent POCO shop?

I doubt it. We don't foresee that any time soon.

What's your favourite food?

Anything Italian. I adore pasta, prawns and garlic bread. I love a Sunday roast too, with crispy potatoes.

Where's the best place for boys' clothes?

M&S or Next. They're good quality and last through all the washes.

Will you design any other clothes?

Yes, that's my plan.

Where do you stay in Portugal?

We've been to loads of different parts all around the Algarve. Since going with the kids we've gone to Quinta do Lago a lot. It ticks all the boxes for us.

CHAPTER TWENTY

Mr and Mrs Ormond

Want to know who's the boss of our house? Or who asked who out first? There's only one way to find out – a Mr and Mrs Quiz!! We both had two cards that said Brian and Pippa on them to hold up for the answers and let's just say we had a lot of fun.

Who is the boss at work?

Brian: She's going to say her, I know she is.

Pippa: I am! But say what you want.

Brian: Pippa. I mean she's going to say it anyway so I may as well say it. She's nicest when she's the boss.

Pippa: I have the final say.

Brian: Pippa makes her decisions. I say, 'What do you think of that? Should I have said that? Should I have done that?' Then we bounce the idea off each other but in the end she always gets her way. Every single time.

Pippa: (laughing, she's really enjoying this) Yeah, obviously I have the final say in everything.

Who is the boss at home?

Pippa: (laughing again) Do you think you are?

Brian: I'm definitely the boss at home.

Pippa: In terms of what though?

Brian: What are you saying? You're the boss full stop?

Pippa: Basically, yeah.

Brian: So basically, we shouldn't do the quiz? Stop the quiz. Every answer is like that.

Pippa: Ha ha! Okay. What do you think you're the boss at home of? We're only on question two and we're going to have a scrap!!

Brian: When it comes to being the boss at home, what areas do you mean?

Pippa: With the kids, I'm the boss but I tell you what you're the boss of. You're the boss of the garden, the light bulbs.

Brian: I don't even do the garden. Okay, well, keep going.

Pippa: Yeah, like handy things around the house. You'd be the boss of anything maintenance-wise.

Brian: Wow, it's all coming out now. I don't do anything at work and I don't do anything at home.

Pippa: Well, I'm the boss of the kids so I decide what they do, when they do it, like activities.

Brian: (laughing now) Can I just check something for a second. Do Pippa's cards say Pippa on both sides? Does she have a Brian one at all?

Who is the most patient?

Pippa: He has no patience whatsoever.

Brian: So it's Pippa again! Oh, it's Pippa again.

Pippa: Sorry, you're the most impatient person. But that's not a bad thing. He's the most impatient person ever, especially when it comes to work because he's such a doer. I'm giving you a compliment now.

Brian: Okay, I take it back. Pippa's definitely the most patient.

Pippa: Yeah, but I mean that in a nice way. Like you are very efficient, everything has to be done now. I would have a bit more patience, you're always on the go.

Who is the biggest messer?

Brian: That's easy.

Pippa: Definitely Brian. He's funnier than me I suppose. He's always playing jokes and he's been telling the same jokes since I've known him. Ha! The same jokes for twelve years. But they're actually your dad's jokes, which is even funnier. When I'm with your dad he

always says, 'Oh, where'd you think he got those jokes?' And you're such a messer. He'll mess with everyone and especially with people that we don't know. We meet someone for the first time and Brian will say something and then they're like, 'What way do I take him?' And I always have to say, 'Take him with a pinch of salt.' It's very funny.

Who is the most fun on a night out?

Brian: She's going to say her, but it's definitely me.

Pippa: Me! I'm the life and soul of the party, let's be honest. I'm the one dancing on the tables, I still think I'm twenty-five.

Brian: If I'm not with Pippa, yes, she'll be the life and soul of the party because she'll go bananas. If I'm there, she'll behave a bit more and I'll be the messer.

Pippa: Do you think?

Brian: Yeah. I'm probably a bit more sensible than you on a night out. I have to drag Pippa away. It's time to go.

Pippa: I never know when enough is enough.

Brian: When I'm there, I'll have loads of craic, but then towards the end of the night, trying to get her to go to bed, forget about it.

Pippa: If someone says it's time to go I get bolshy. We will not go!

Brian: You've already had enough Pippa, we've got to go.

Pippa: That's the worst thing you could say to me.

Brian: Is 'who's the most stubborn' a question?!

Pippa: I think we've all had enough now. Who's had enough? Not me!

Who is the most stubborn?

Brian: We are both very stubborn, but I think you win the watch on that one.

Pippa: I'd say 50/50.

Brian: Not a chance, 60/40.

Pippa: I'm a bit softer than you Brian. I say you, you say me. We're
          both Leos, so . . .

Brian: See, I told you she was stubborn.

Pippa: (laughing) We're both very alike. I don't know how this has lasted
          as long as it has.

Brian: Neither do I.

And who is the tidiest?

Brian: Oh now this one is too easy.

Pippa: I'm not tidy at all.

Brian: When Pippa opens her post, it's like Christmas morning. And she'll
          go to different areas of the house, so there might be a bag in one
          room and she'll take everything out, leave it there and walk
          away into the kitchen to open another one.

Pippa: I'd have wrappers everywhere. I do it now just to piss you off
          because you go mad.

Brian: No you don't, because you don't even know you're doing it.

Who is the most romantic?

Brian: That's a tough one but I'm definitely going with me on that one.
          All I think about is what we're going to do.

Pippa: Yeah, you would be.

Brian: Because I care a little bit more.

Pippa: Ah no, stop! But you are good at thinking ahead and
          planning things.

Brian: You were very good but I think you've kind of dipped a little.

Pippa: That's because your fortieth is coming up and I'm panicking. What am I doing?

Brian: The good thing about this is that Pippa sets the standard for her fortieth with mine!

Pippa: That won't be for a very long time, so don't you worry.

Who is the best cook?

Brian: If Pippa puts her mind to it, she is definitely the best cook.

Pippa: Yeah. I can cook, if I put my mind to it.

Brian: You'd have no problem opening a book and cooking from scratch.

Pippa: Yeah, I could. I like adding ingredients, but I don't really do it often. It doesn't come naturally to me.

Brian: I would disagree. I think it comes very naturally to you.

Pippa: Ah thanks. Actually, that's the big secret. I took a break from the Fashion Factories so I could stay home and cook for Brian!

Brian: Husband factory! That's our new thing.

Who made the first move?

Brian: We're both going to say the opposite person, but it was definitely Pippa.

Pippa: Oh hello, as if.

Brian: I don't want to make her look bad so I'll say it was me.

Pippa: You made the first move.

Brian: Oh did I?

Pippa: Yeah, I remember you coming up to me in Krystal which is even a bit more embarrassing because you were sober.

Brian: So I just walked up to you sober?

Pippa: Well we'd had our picture taken by Brian McEvoy outside.

Brian: Thank you, we had already been introduced.

Pippa: But then when we went in, into the bar area, you said something, you basically asked for my number. You made the first move. He did, he did.

Brian: Who was the sober one?

Pippa: You did ask for it. We were talking about TV presenting because you were doing *You're a Star* the next day and you said, 'If you want any advice, here's my number.' You did.

Brian: You really think that?

Pippa: That is one hundred per cent true.

Brian: Then Pippa goes on to say, 'I totally forgot I even met you that night. Then I was watching the telly, and thought oh that's the Brian I met.'

Pippa: I did. That's true.

Brian: That's really how drunk she was.

Pippa: No – or how not-memorable you were.

Brian: Throw on a few years and she married him.

Who planned the first date?

Brian: It ended up being a double date, didn't it?

Pippa: Yeah, but you would have asked me.

Brian: Well I am the most romantic, so it probably was me. We ended up going for dinner with Laura Woods and her new boyfriend who is now her husband, Mark.

Pippa: No, our actual double date was when we went to the Gaiety Theatre to some show. There were a few people there. Then Mark and Laura Woods just happened to be in the restaurant.

Brian: Yeah, we walked into the Unicorn and there was Laura and Mark on one of their first dates. So we sort of crashed their Valentine's Day.

Pippa: Yeah. Which was a nice little icebreaker for us.

Who planned the last date you were on?

Pippa: What was our last date? Dinner in Sallins.

Brian: Oh yeah, I booked that. Again, I'm the most romantic.

Who would Ollie and Louis say is the boss?

Brian: Probably Pippa. Would you say you?

Pippa: Yeah. Because you always say, 'Ask your mama, she's the boss.' You say that to them.

Brian: Yeah, so it's Pippa.

Pippa: The boys would think I'm stricter. They look to you for fun, they probably think you're softer, more of a messer.

That's it!

Pippa: Oh thank God, we're still intact for now.

Brian: Want to go on a date tonight?

Pippa: Aww!

THANK YOU!

When my first book was released in October 2016, I never in a million years thought I'd even get to that point, never mind be here doing it all over again. The success of the first one still amazes me and I'm still as emotional bringing this one to life as I was the first time round.

One thing's for sure, I wouldn't be in this position if it wasn't for my loyal following. I feel like I've grown up with so many of you following along from day one. I'm eternally grateful for your support and encouragement in all that I do.

A whole lot has changed and evolved in my life in three years and I knew I had another book to give, I just wasn't sure if I could make it happen to be honest. I now have another little man in my life and an ever-growing business. When Claire Pelly came to me and said 'are you ready to do another' I thought to myself, I'd love to but realistically how!

I was reassured by Claire and the Penguin team that they'd have my back and help in every way to make it happen. That's exactly what they did. I got to work with the most amazing team. Professionals really make things look easy, when really we all know nothing is easy – they're just really good at their jobs. So thank you so very much Claire Pelly, Michael McLoughlin, Abi Hartshorne and the extended team at Penguin.

I owe a massive thank you to Jen Stevens who helped me put my words on paper. I wouldn't have been able to do it without you. I love your 'no problem' approach to everything. Thank you for understanding me and my sense of humour. Little did I know all those years ago when you gave me my first column that we'd be working together again today. Thank you for being so deadly and easy-going!

There were lots of other superwomen who contributed to making this book happen – all women I love and work with on an ongoing basis.

Lili Forberg and Laoise Moggan – two unbelievably talented photographers.

Laura Warren Tracey for doing anything that's needed at any time to keep the show on the road.

Niamh Doherty, my little fashionista.

Orla Neligan, thank you for having the most creative eye and bringing things to life!

To my sister Susanna – thank you for being an integral part of this exciting rollercoaster we are on. I'm so lucky to have you involved and so grateful that you care as much as I do.

To the two most important little men in my life. Ollie and Louis, thank you for making me a determined working Mama. It's not always easy keeping all the balls in the air but you two make it all worthwhile. I'm so proud of you both and I hope you'll grow up being proud of me too.

To Brian, my husband, partner in everything I do and my best friend. Thank you for always encouraging me, for guiding me and for keeping me going. I feel like I can do anything when I'm with you.

Finally my guardian angel and Mum Lulu, I now know you're always with me and guiding me to where I'm meant to be.

Xx